AF599264

ALONG THE OLD DARLINGTON ROAD

A HISTORY OF THE DARLINGTON ROAD VALLEY, MINERAL POINT, WISCONSIN

JOHN C. SHARP, JR.

Little Creek Press.
5341 Sunny Ridge Road
Mineral Point, WI 53565

ORDERING INFORMATION
Quantity sales. Special discounts are available on quantity purchases by corporations, associations, and others. For details, contact info@littlecreekpress.com

Orders by US trade bookstores and wholesalers.
Please contact Little Creek Press or Ingram for details.

Printed in the United States of America

Cataloging-in-Publication Data
Names: Sharp, John C., author.
Title: Along the Old Darlington Road / John C. Sharp, Jr.
Description: Mineral Point, WI: Little Creek Press, 2023
Identifiers: LCCN: 2023923018 | ISBN: 978-1-955656-68-9
Subjects:
HIS036010 HISTORY / United States / State & Local / General
HIS036090 HISTORY / United States / State & Local / Midwest
HIS036040 HISTORY / United States / 19th Century

Book design by Little Creek Press

CONTENTS

ACKNOWLEDGMENTS

There are many Mineral Pointers to thank far and wide for their input into this interesting history. First and foremost, my thanks to Nancy Pfotenhauer. Nancy was curator of the Mineral Point Library Archives from 2015 to 2020, and her knowledge of Mineral Point history has been an inspiration to me. She has given me encouragement from beginning to end. Her seminar on using Chronicling America provided me with my most valuable research tool.

Past curators Liz Holmes and Mary Alice Moore and current curators Shan Thomas and Joel Gosse have all been in on the project. Their professionalism at the archives has been a help to many people besides myself.

Love and gratitude to my wife, Jennifer, for the conversations, encouragement, and assistance she has given.

Other valuable resources have been the Wisconsin Department of Transportation, Iowa County Road Department, the Southwest Wisconsin Room at UW-Platteville, Iowa County Recorder's Office and the Town of Mineral Point road ledger and Town minutes, so graciously made available to me by Debi Heisner, Mineral Point Town Clerk.

Thanks as well to Mineral Pointers Dean Keyes, Carl Tunestam, Paul Whitford and the Whitford family, Paul Fine, Ruth Jungbluth, Rose Filardo Temple, Adam and Ted Landon, Bob McNeill, Jr., Larry Ross, Terry Poad, Mike Gratz, Parmely Harris, Jim Harris, the Jerry Walsh family, Catherine Whitford, and Lois Holland.

Hopefully this research will preserve the history of this little valley and the businesses that located here from the earliest beginnings of Mineral Point to the present. Any blunders of fact or context are solely my own.

John Sharp

INTRODUCTION

This circa 1915 photo taken from 4th Street in Mineral Point shows the Darlington Road crossing over Mineral Point Creek on its way east. Just before coming to the Mineral Point Town Hall, the road forked north to Dodge Street and the Merry Christmas Mine building. The main road made a long, uphill, sweeping curve to the south toward the Graysville Community and Darlington.

My interest in the Old Darlington Road area began when my wife, Jennifer, discovered and purchased the east end of the old Keith Mitchell Salvage Yard from Ted Landon in 1997. By this time all of the junk car bodies and other metal had been crushed and hauled away, and shoulder-high Queen Anne's Lace and white clover were growing everywhere. The one thing that caught her attention was a beautiful small stream winding its way along the base of the hillside. Jennifer thought that even though this property had been a salvage yard from the 1920s until the 1980s, it could be restored back to its original beauty with some hard work and tender loving care. Today, the property is designated as a Certified Wildlife Habitat by the National Wildlife Federation. She was right, the property was indeed a diamond in the rough.

Mineral Point Library Archives

Mitchell Salvage Yard, circa 1980

We were attracted to this land for many reasons. Two stood out the most: its close proximity to town and the beautiful small stream that ran along the bottom of the hillside. These aspects of the land, location and water attracted us, and for that matter had attracted many others before us. Little did we know that an important part of Mineral Point's early commercial history had played out in this small valley along Old Darlington Road. Location and water have basically determined its use and history from the early days of Mineral Point.

To help reclaim and restore the land, we had 2,000 cubic yards of clay dirt hauled in to cover and contour the old salvage yard. Once the dirt was graded and contoured to our liking, the city began bringing us truckloads of leaves every fall, which we composted to help build better soil. By 2003, Jennifer and I had the land pretty much cleaned up and graded, and we began planting trees and bushes to restore its beauty.

Having an interest in history, several features on or near our property made me curious as to what had transpired in this valley over the years. There was a very old rock quarry on the hillside to the south of us, and nearby to the west, there was a huge brick chimney and an old railroad bed with the remains of wooden bridge pilings where trains had once crossed the creek. I also heard that a mill pond once covered most of the salvage yard.

Left: Looking west down Mineral Point Creek. John Sharp, 2008. Right: Delivery of clay dirt. John Sharp, 1997

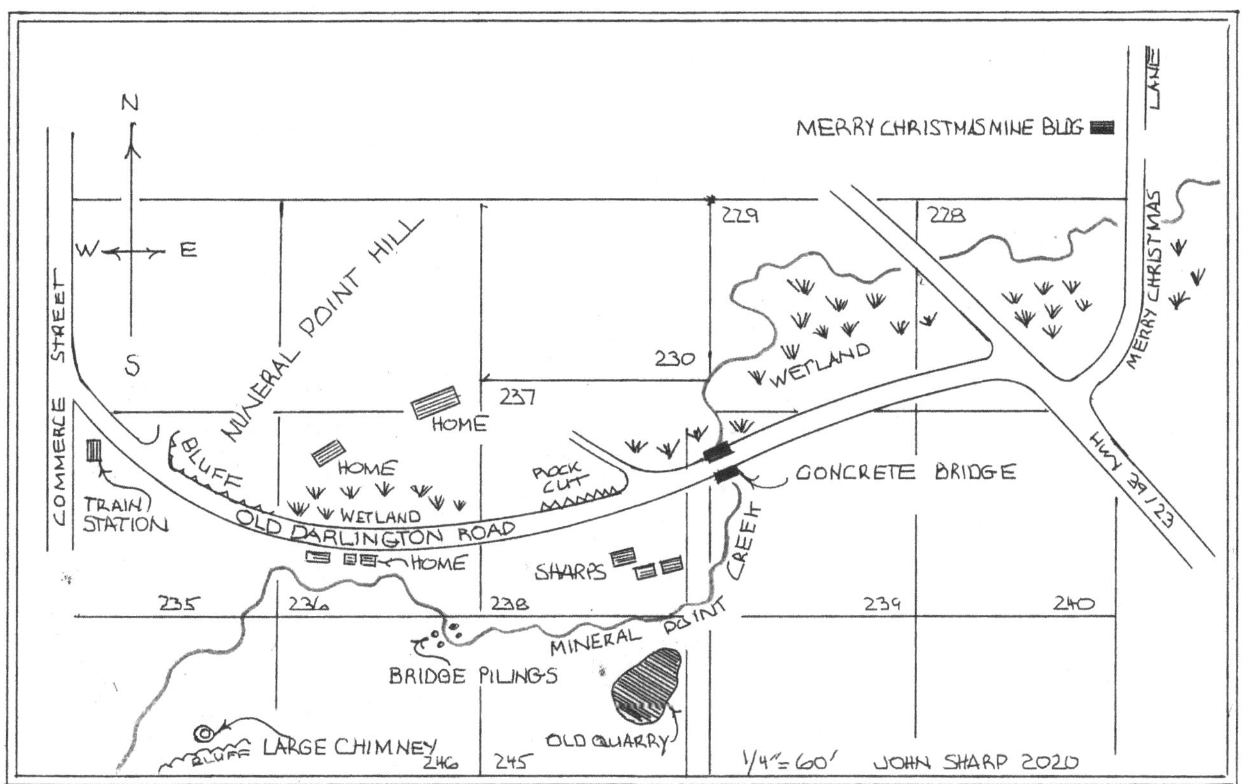

Old Darlington Road, 2020. Map drawn by John Sharp.

One evening while talking with Parmely Harris at a Mineral Point Historical Society meeting, Parm told me his grandfather, Jim Harris, had immigrated to Mineral Point from England in the early 1850s. Jim was a hauler, and he was looking for work. At this time, the Mineral Point Railroad Depot was under construction, and Jim landed a job as a drayman, hauling stone from the old quarry on our property to build the depot. Upon learning this information from Parm, I began calling the old quarry the "Depot Quarry."

View of the old Depot Quarry. John Sharp 1998

The information about Parm's grandfather piqued my interest in the Old Darlington Road valley, so I decided to expand my research of the valley to cover not only our property, but to cover the area from the Mineral Point Railroad Depot to the Merry Christmas Mine building, a distance of around 1/2 mile.

Where should I start looking for answers to my many questions? I knew the Mineral Point Library had historical archives dealing with Mineral Point's history. I went there first and have been a regular visitor for the past several years. In 1980, a portion of the old library building was dedicated to collecting Mineral Point history. It was housed in the old jail section of the library's basement and was called the

Mineral Point Room. When the library was remodeled in 2011, the Mineral Point Room was moved out of the basement jail area and up to the old council chambers on the top floor. It is now called the Mineral Point Library Archives, and it is a beautiful, sunny room in which to do research. Important and interesting information having to do with Mineral Point has been saved there over the years, and it is truly a treasure trove of Mineral Point history.

Mineral Point has been fortunate to have some dedicated and serious women managing the historical collection from its inception. They have all been knowledgeable of the collections and have always gone above and beyond to help interested amateur historians such as myself find what they are looking for. I sought help on my research from Liz Holmes, Mary Alice Moore, Nancy Pfotenhauer and Shan Thomas.

Other excellent resources for historical research that I have used include the Southwest Wisconsin Room, Platteville, Wisconsin; UW Historical Society, Madison, Wisconsin; State Department of Transportation, Madison, Wisconsin; County Recorder's Office, Dodgeville, Wisconsin; Town of Mineral Point; Library of Congress, Chronicling America site, and last but not least, local "Mineral Pointers."

I have been fascinated to learn how much has transpired in this little valley since 1828. Not only was the Darlington Road valley the site of a salvage yard and an old rock quarry, but it was the site of the first flour mill and first woolen mill in Mineral Point. These businesses located in the valley because of the stream and its potential for water power. Other businesses that located in the valley were the Badger Rubber Works, the Mineral Point Concrete Construction Company, a tallow factory and a leather tannery. Those businesses all needed water. In addition to those businesses, the Mineral Point and Northern Railroad Company built a spur up the valley in 1904 that ended right in our front yard. And to make my search even more interesting, I learned that Mineral Point's most famous and colorful, first full-time female resident, Matilda Hood, was the original owner of much of the valley, including our land, which she received in land patents from the federal government on March 3, 1837.

Matilda Hood. Mineral Point Library Archive

CHAPTER 1: HISTORY OF THE ROAD

What today is Old Darlington Road begins at its intersection with Commerce Street near the old Mineral Point Railroad Depot. Running due east for 1/2 mile, the road runs up a small valley that is a natural corridor to and from Mineral Point. The valley is flanked by sandstone bluffs on either side of its entrance, and as it continues up the valley, the road rounds the southern tip of Mineral Point Hill, passes wetlands and rocky outcroppings, crosses Mineral Point Creek and ends at Highway 39/23.

Before Highway 39/23 was built in 1949, Old Darlington Road was known only as "Darlington Road." It forked near the old Mineral Point Town Hall. The smaller left-hand fork dropped off the hillside and continued east toward Dodge Street, now known as Merry Christmas Lane. The main road continued up the hill, made a wide turn to the south and proceeded on to Darlington.

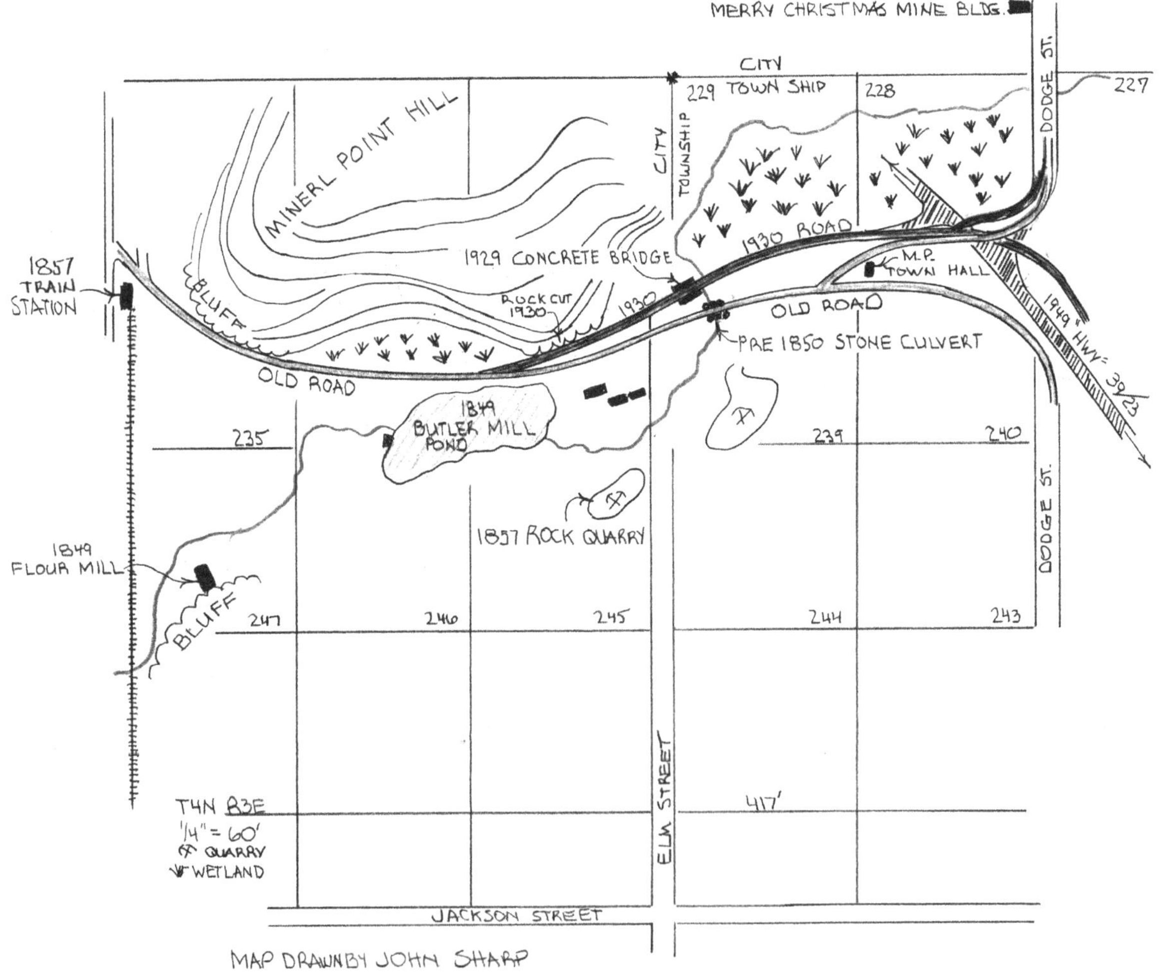

The "Old Road" on the previous map roughly shows the earliest route taken by Darlington Road as it crossed over Mineral Point Creek on an old stone culvert and then made a big sweeping uphill curve to the south. The "1930 Road" shows how the road was straightened and shifted to the north in 1929, when a new concrete bridge was built. In 1949, Highway 39/23 was built, and it became the main road into Mineral Point from the south and east, and Darlington Road became known as "Old Darlington Road."

Since the earliest days of Mineral Point, Darlington Road had been the main road east out of the city for travelers on their way to the Graysville farming and mining community, Hollandale, Darlington, and even Chicago. The 1871 Taylor and Willets map labels it as "ROAD." The 1872 Bird's Eye View map labels it "Grayville Road." Over the years, it has also been known as the "Darlington Mineral Point Highway," "State Trunk Highway 62" and "Highway 23," but it has been mainly known as the Darlington Road.

This 1871 Taylor and Willets map shows the early surveyed and platted streets of Spring Street, Elm Street, Jackson Street and Dodge Street. Darlington Road, which was not surveyed or platted originally, was added to the map at a later date and was labeled "ROAD." Spring Street and Elm Street were never opened. Spring Street has been abandoned by the city. Dodge Street has become known as Merry Christmas Lane.

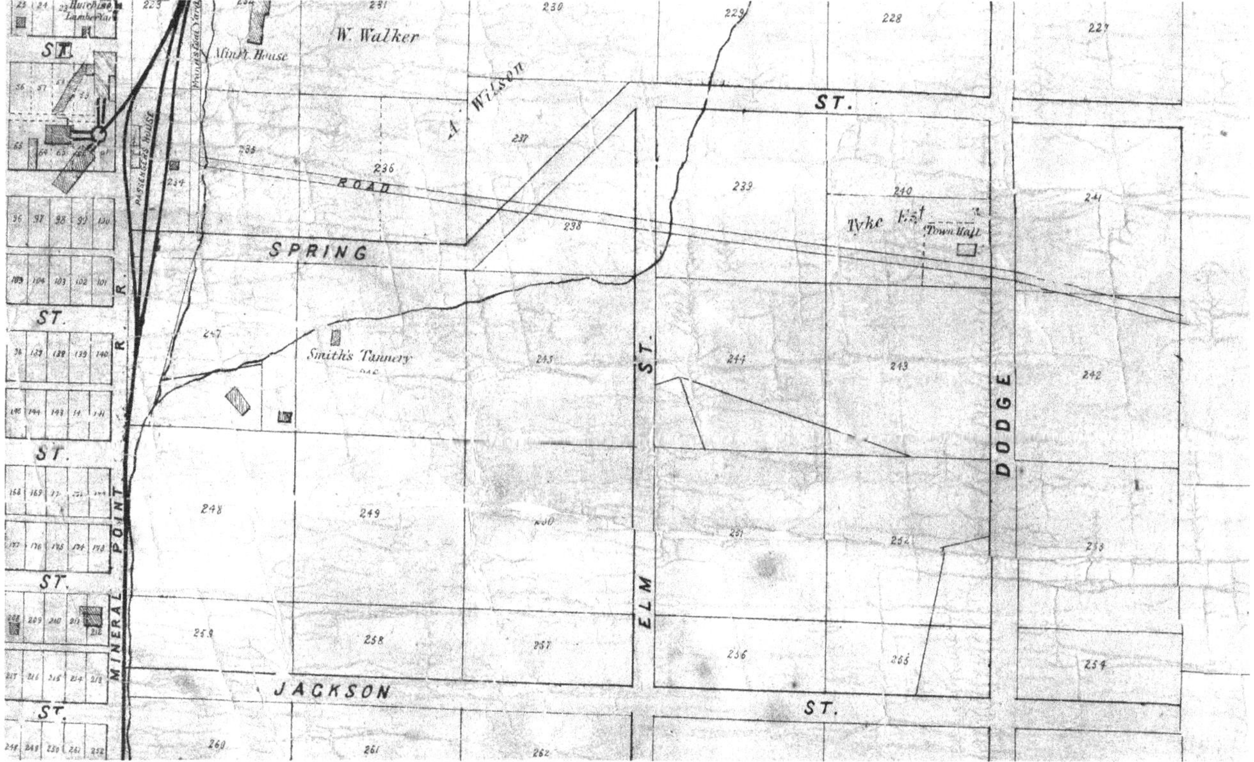

1871 Taylor and Willets Map. Mineral Point Library Archives

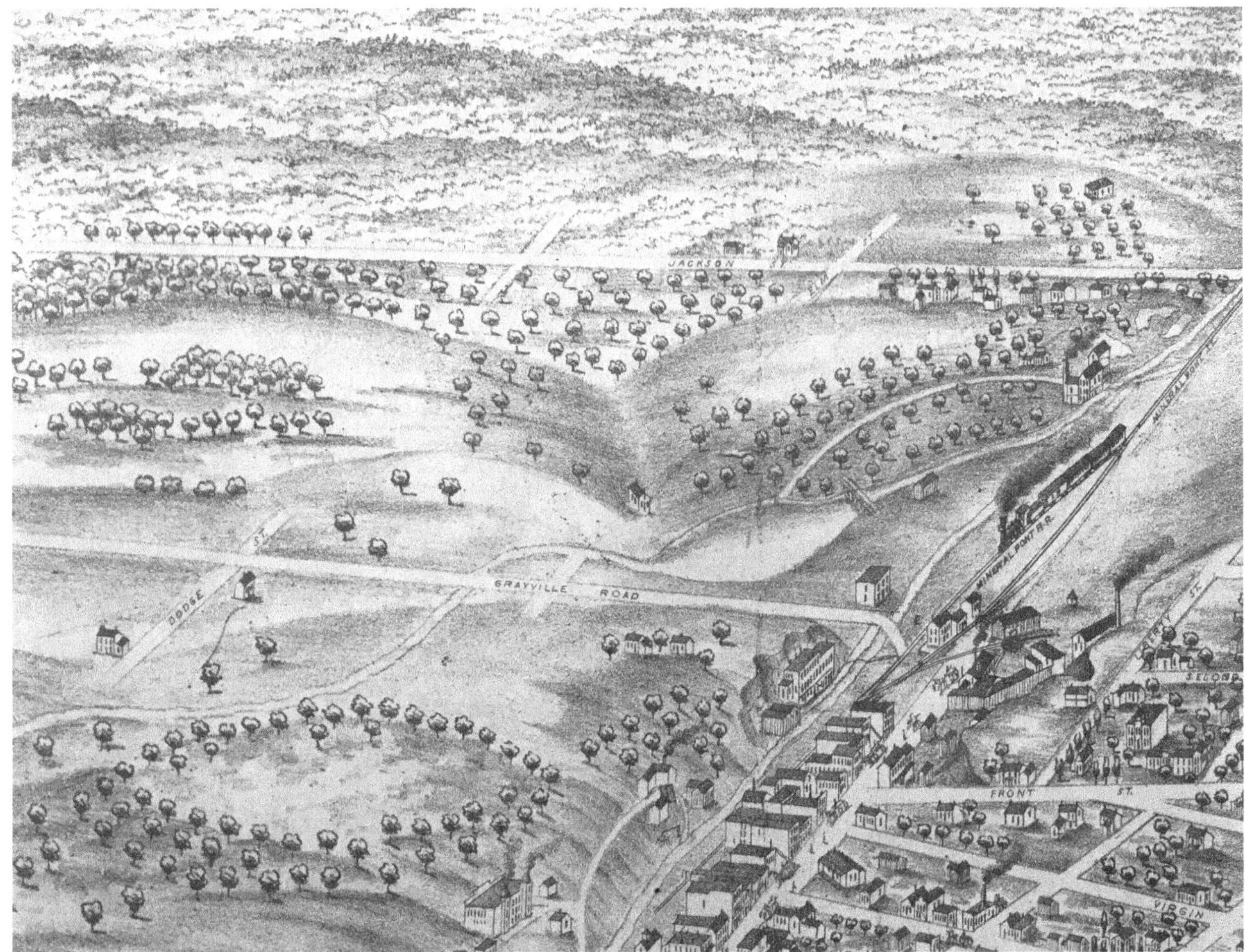

1872 Bird's Eye View Map. Mineral Point Library Archives

I like to think that Darlington Road was originally an Indian trail, as many roads once were. It is well known that Native Americans had been coming to the "Point" to dig and smelt lead in crude furnaces well before Mineral Point was settled. As early as the 1600s, lead was mined and used by the Indians to make trinkets and as a trade item with the French. Surely the Indians traveled down the small valley where Darlington Road is located to obtain lead, pick berries and drink from its clear, cool springs.

An article in the May 29, 1867 issue of the *Mineral Point Weekly Tribune* talks of the Winnebagos taking their annual trip to this area and camping near the Musgrove furnace, which was located in the vicinity of what today is known as the Merry Christmas Mine building, and Chief Evergreen Tree from Wisconsin Dells, as told by William N. Hawke, Catherine Whitford's father, brought his people to this area as late as 1960 to pick the plentiful wild berries that still grow here.

Indian trails and old roads are sometimes mentioned in early land surveys. In 1833, Wisconsin created the Wisconsin Public Land Survey. This survey was conducted by the federal government's General Land Office, and it was divided into two parts. The "exterior survey" divided the land into townships.

The "interior survey" established section and quarter-section boundaries within townships. These surveys were recorded in small notebooks, and the interior survey often gave a brief description of the land surface, quality of the soil, tree species and other dominant features. I wondered if it would show Darlington Road as an early road or Indian trail in the valley. By looking at plat maps, I determined that the Darlington Road area I am interested in is located in the NW ¼ of Section 5, Township 4 north, range 3 east. Thus, I was hoping some details of a trail or early road would be mentioned.

The page at left from the 1833 "Interior Survey" describes the land *"Between Section 5 & 6 as rather uneven & 1st rate—being thinly timbered with oak, with a brook running southwest and fresh diggings."* Unfortunately, there was no mention of a trail or road in this survey.

When the town grew, the trail most likely grew along with it. First it was an oxen and horse trail, then a wagon road and finally an improved automobile road.

Early road-building equipment included a team of horses, scrapers and plows, shovels and a split-log drag. Dirt roads pretty much had to follow the contours of the land. Maintenance of these roads was minimal. When it rained, or in the spring thaw, they turned into quagmires.

This horse-drawn Fresno scraper is an example of early road-building equipment.

Wisconsin State Historical Society

Some time prior to 1850, the Town of Mineral Point built what was called a "culvert" over Mineral Point Creek on Darlington Road. It was more like a bridge. The materials used to construct this culvert were beautifully cut limestone blocks from a local quarry. The culvert was so well built, that it remained in use until 1929, a period of 79-plus years.

The following field notes were obtained from the Town of Mineral Point road ledger. They refer to the road (Highway 23) built from Mineral Point to the Lafayette County line. The first field note records the date of survey. The second is a portion of the field notes and plat done to the Mineral Point Creek culvert and the third entry shows a portion of the original map that was drawn for this road.

Surveyed June 29. 1850. by A. W. Comfort

Field Notes and Plat

Of the Survey of a Road from where Commerce Street crosses the Township line in Mineral Point to Lafayette County line

Courses		Distance	Remarks
South		2.60	
S 25½°	E.	8.40	
" 83°	"	4.50	
" 86½°	"	8.50	To Telegraph Post
N 71°	E	8.50	Culvert at the end of 6 50/100 chains

Township Line

Culvert

1 Mile

Center of Sec. 5

4

By the 1900s, bigger and newer equipment such as tractors, graders, steam shovels and dump wagons made it possible to straighten roads and cut through rock outcroppings and hills. Bad turns, steep grades and rocky roads were eliminated due to this new equipment. Dirt roads were being macadamized, which was a type of road construction developed around 1820 by a Scottish road engineer named John Loudon McAdam. This method of road building used small single-sized, angular crushed stone layers placed in shallow lifts and compacted thoroughly to create a firm surface.

Iowa County Democrat, November 18, 1915

> That portion of the Darlington Road lying in the city limits of Mineral Point has been regraded and surfaced with macadam. It has long been in bad condition, and the improvement will be greatly appreciated by the public.

This crushed rock was quarried in local quarries around the city. Major improvements continued on Darlington Road up until 1948.

In 1916, President Woodrow Wilson signed the Federal Aid Highway Act. It offered direct aid to states for building and improving their highways. This act helped Wisconsin create its state trunk highway system in 1917. Darlington Road was designated as part of this system and became known as Highway 62. State Trunk Highway 62 ran from Highway 11 south of Darlington, through Mineral Point on the Darlington Road and then on to Edmond, where it ended. These numbered highways improved on the old named trail system and made it much easier for travelers to find their way. The public generally wanted wider and better roads because of the increased use of the automobile. Even with the new Highway 62 designation, local residents continued to refer to STH-62 as Darlington Road or the Darlington Mineral Point Highway.

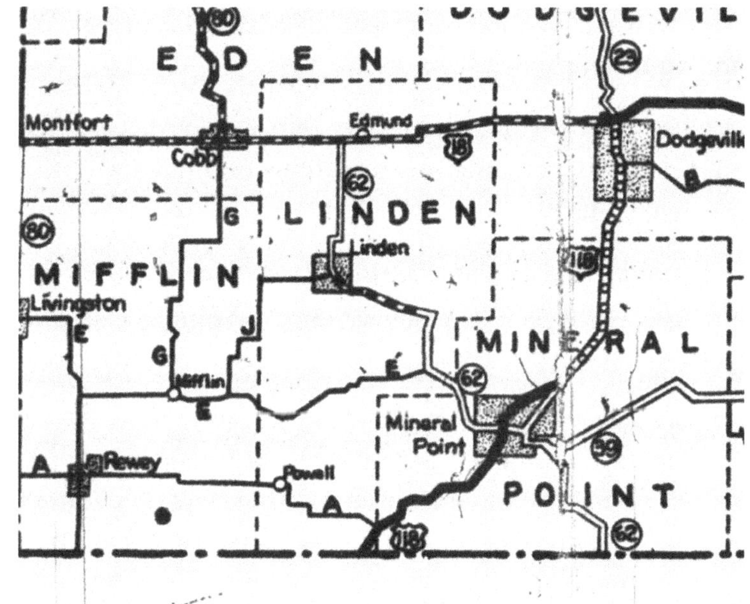

The sharp uphill turn on Darlington Road near the old town hall was always a challenge and troublesome for wagons and early vehicles. The following articles make mention of this issue.

Iowa County Democrat, July 1, 1915

Another good piece of work has been done by the town on Darlington Road near the site of the old town hall. The road on the hillside there has long been very hard to climb, but it is now greatly improved.

Iowa County Democrat, November 23, 1922

ROAD CONSTRUCTION NEARING CITY

The Lampert Construction Company is now working on one of the last laps on their work on the Darlington Road. This week a big steam shovel was used in breaking the ground near the site of the old town hall where the new road will be made. The long winding turn on the hill at this place will be avoided by a straight cut through the pasture adjoining it on the left-hand side.

Even with these improvements, the big turn and hill past the old town hall site remained a challenge.

Paul Whitford

Paul Whitford of Mineral Point, who hauled hogs and cattle from the stock corrals on Darlington Road to Chicago and Milwaukee for the Ross Brother's Trucking Company in the 1940s, had some choice names of his own for the Darlington Road hill. He told me that making it around the big turn by the old town hall site and up the hill was always a bear for the stock trucks. After several colorful words of encouragement, he was always relieved to get over that hill and on his way.

In 1929, the old stone bridge over Mineral Point Creek, as beautiful and well-built as it was, outlasted its usefulness and gave way to a newer and larger concrete bridge.

Iowa County Democrat, November 7, 1929

P. J. DUNLAP COMPANY STARTS WORK ON CONSTRUCTION OF NEW BRIDGE

The P. J. Dunlap Construction company of Mt. Horeb has been hauling material and machinery, a quarter mile east of Mineral Point on Highway 62, preparatory to building a new bridge in order to straighten the highway. The bridge will be a thirty-foot span. A portion of the crew has been on the job for the past ten days erecting a derrick and digging for a foundation. Difficulty has been encountered in getting a good bottom for the foundation. It is probable that piles will be driven in order to insure a good foundation. The contract is let at $22.50 a yard. The bridge will be located about seventy-five feet north of the present road, and a fill of about four feet will be made for a distance of from seven to eight hundred feet. It is not likely, however, that the road will be straightened before spring.

John Sharp 2018

Darlington Road (STH 62) and Mineral Point would be getting a new concrete bridge over Mineral Point Creek.

In order to build this new bridge, the road needed to be relocated to the north and straightened. To do this, Iowa County purchased a curved strip of land 4 rods wide from the Mineral Point Zinc Company. This strip of land was approximately 75 feet north of the center line of what was then the old rock bridge on Darlington Road. This sale took place on June 17, 1929, for the consideration of $175.20. (Conveyance of Land for Highway Purposes (Sec. 83.08) Vol. 131 Deeds, page 170.)

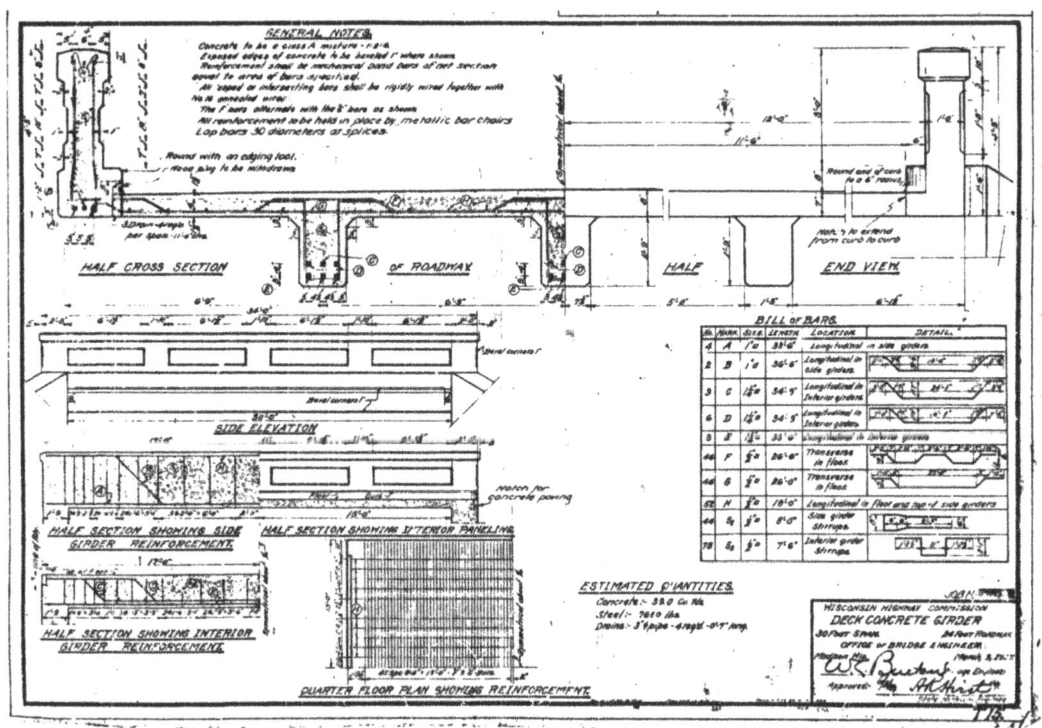

Blueprint used for the construction of the new concrete bridge over Mineral Point Creek.
Iowa County Road Department, Dodgeville Wisconsin.

Iowa County Democrat, April 17, 1930

A crew began work Monday relocating and grading up to the new concrete bridge on Highway 62 on the outskirts of this city. Dave Williams, a county foreman, is in charge of this work at Butler's Dam.

When the new concrete bridge was built, the old stone culvert was left in place, and all but the very top of the bridge was buried. Its top rocks are still visible today (shown at right).

On July 13th, 1948, Wisconsin Governor Rennebohm approved a contract between the State Highway Commission and the Dixon Construction Company of Albany, Wisconsin, to build a new road from the Highway 39/23 intersection ("Graysville Corner") to the junction of Commerce, Doty and Hoard Streets ("Five Points") in Mineral Point. Coming into the city on Darlington Road was considered unsatisfactory since it was narrow and poorly aligned. When the new highway was completed, it would bypass Darlington Road and make a huge cut through the Mineral Point Hill. When the new highway opened in July, 1949, Darlington Road was bypassed and would no longer be the main road into Mineral Point. From 1949 to this day, Darlington Road would be known as "Old Darlington Road."

Iowa County Democrat, September 23, 1948

CONSTRUCTION CO. AT WORK ON MINERAL POINT HILL

The Dixon Construction Company started uncovering the rock on the Mineral Point Hill Saturday. Two large dirt movers powered by Caterpillar tractors are taking the soil from the surface of the hill to the bottom near the old Thrasher Pond. The rock will be crushed later and used for road foundation on the Iowa County end of Highway 23. The angle at which the big tractors ply up and down the hill is close to 45 degrees, steep enough to worry the large group of onlookers watching the operation daily.

Highway 39/23 being bulldozed through Mineral Point Hill. Mineral Point Library Archives

An interesting aside to Darlington Road history and the new highway being built occurred when the Dixon Construction Company uncovered a large vein of lead and zinc ore as they made the huge cut through the Mineral Point Hill.

Striking lead and zinc in this new cut on the Mineral Point Hill was not surprising. According to the "1881 History of Iowa County," the Mineral Point Hill gained fame in 1828 when Nat MorrIs and two fellow prospectors made a significant discovery of lead ore there. News of that discovery spread fast, and the rush for "Grey Gold" was on. Overnight, Mineral Point became the most important community situated in the heart of the lead region.

News of this modern-day discovery also spread fast, and it gained fame when the United Press News Agency got wind of it and wired it to all parts of the county. This story appeared in the *Wisconsin State Journal* and was reprinted in the September 30, 1948 *Iowa County Democrat.*

> **RUSH IS ON AS KIDS GRAB FOR TREASURE**
>
> Mineral Point—(U. P.)
>
> Small-fry treasure hunters pushed over the trail to Mineral Point Hill today with the battle cry: "There's gold in that there hill!"
>
> They were armed with picks and shovels. They carried buckets and bags and baskets—anything to carry away valuable ore. They had the fever bad, just like 49ers of California.
>
> **BULLDOZER DOES IT**
>
> The rush of 1948 began when bulldozers tore into the side of the hill to make way for Highway 23. The giant blades turned up tons of lead and zinc ore worth something like $17 a hundred pounds. (That would be equal to $182 in 2020 money.)
>
> **"CANDY FOR A YEAR"**
>
> As the news spread, the imaginative boys of Mineral Point forgot all about their homework and hit the trail. Old Peter Quier, a veteran miner, protested that he had the rights to all the ore. But he had to fall into line when the state announced it owned the land. The young prospectors are carrying their treasure to the Dodgeville Mining Co. and pocketing enough spending money to buy candy for a year. One boy netted $25.50. Next target of the bulldozers is the "Merry Christmas," a famous abandoned surface mine. The youngsters can't wait to move in on another strike."

Tom Marr (center) and buddies looking for pieces of lead ore on the 1948 road construction site as it entered Mineral Point. The boys sold some of the lead ore they found to Dave Fine at his Darlington Road salvage yard for spending money. Mineral Point Library Archives.

CHAPTER 2: EARLY BEGINNINGS

One of the first people mentioned in the early history of Mineral Point is Nat Morris. According to the "1881 History of Iowa County," he and two fellow prospectors arrived in the area in 1828 and made a significant discovery of lead on Mineral Point Hill. This began the development of Mineral Point as the commercial hub of the lead and zinc mining region.

Southwest Wisconsin was government-reserved Indian lands when the prospectors and other settlers first came to southwest Wisconsin. They were considered trespassers and squatters on any Indian-reserved lands they occupied. If they wanted to file a squatter's claim on their mines or land holdings they could not do so until after August 1, 1829, when Winnebago lands were ceded to the United States Government in the Treaty of Prairie du Chien.

After the Winnebago lands had been ceded, the federal General Land Office began surveying and dividing southwest Wisconsin into townships and sections. Once this land survey was completed, and a land office established in Mineral Point in 1834, public lands not excluded from sale, such as school lands, were offered for sale. Squatters could then claim their "squatter's rights" and file a preemption certificate which would give them first right to purchase the land they had developed at a federally set minimum price rather than compete with land speculators at bidding auctions. To claim "squatter's rights" a squatter had to have constructed buildings, put up fences for livestock, cleared land for planting small gardens and growing crops or develop the land in other ways.

A final land purchase could be executed with a land patent which was the initial specific transfer of land titles from the federal government to individuals. The possibility of getting legal title to land gave settlers the impetus they needed to further develop their lands and begin farming and other ventures in a serious way.

Of the thousands of miners who swarmed into the lead region, very few had success with mining. Many miners who did not achieve the riches they had hoped for moved on. Those who stayed filed land claims and turned to other types of work such as farming.

In the early mining years, the government prohibited the development of Wisconsin's rich agriculture land as a way of forcing miners to devote full time to mining. In an effort to get more variety and better greens, small gardens were grown where possible. By 1832, people were so starved for quality food that the superintendent of the mining country stopped enforcing the restriction on land cultivation so those who wanted to farm could do so. Early Wisconsin settlers who shifted to farming as a livelihood often chose wheat as a crop because it had a low initial planting cost and a relative high rate of return. By the 1850s, wheat had become a major agricultural crop in Iowa County.

With all the wheat being grown, a grist mill to grind it into flour was of exceptional importance to the farmers and citizens of the area. Mineral Point did not have a functioning grist mill that could grind this wheat into bolted flour for domestic use until 1857. Flour for baking was purchased in Galena or Milwaukee at exceptionally high prices. Farmers had to travel great distances by horse and wagon to get their grains to a mill for grinding. The following article reflected this situation.

> ### *Mineral Point Tribune*, January 27, 1853
>
> There is perhaps, no community in our county so destitute in this particular as Mineral Point and its vicinity. Our farmers have now to go from 10 to 15 or even 20 miles to a mill, and then very often leave their grain and go after it again another day.

A grist mill had been built east of Mineral Point on Mineral Point Creek in the 1830s. It was a small mill and could only grind corn meal and animal feed. Its mill stones were not made to grind wheat into flour for home baking. Residents of the county continued to buy baking flour in Galena and Milwaukee. The small log mill was in operation for only a few years and its mill stones have been saved and archived with the Mineral Point Historical Society at Orchard Lawn in Mineral Point.

Building a grist mill in or near Mineral Point became extremely important. Thus, it is no surprise that in 1845, plans were formulated to build a mill within the city limits on Mineral Point Creek. The new grist mill would be built against the south bluff as you enter the Darlington Road valley. It would be one of the first commercial enterprises along the creek within the city.

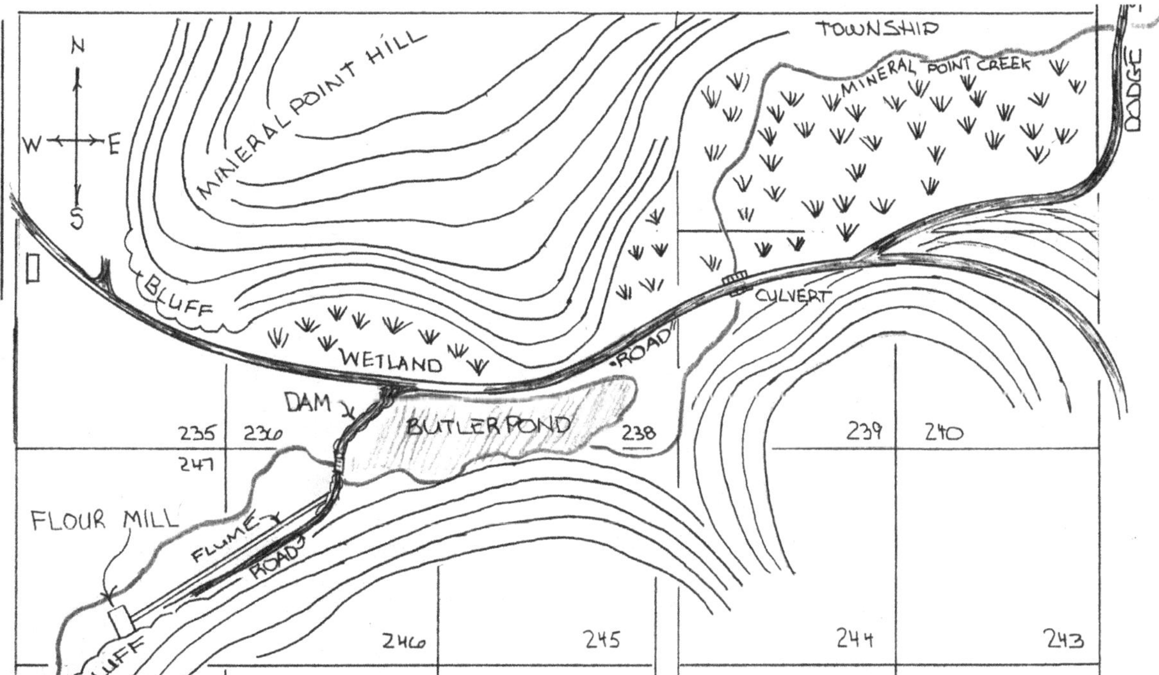

This map shows the Mineral Point City Mill located between Mineral Point Creek and the south bluff entrance to the Darlington Road valley. John Sharp 2020

Mineral Point Creek begins as a small spring about two miles east of Mineral Point on the old Stan and Lois Holland farm. As the creek winds its way in a southwesterly direction down the valley towards Mineral Point, it is fed by several more springs. Then it is joined by Brewery Creek near the Mineral Point City Mill and continues its journey southward. Its watershed encompasses around 2,000 acres and is defined by Highway 39 on the south, just east of "CTH D" on the east and Antoine Road on the north. The creek is not a large creek by any measure, but large enough to turn a water wheel and supply power for a grist mill.

The name of the Mineral Point Creek has changed through the years. An 1862 Geological Survey of the State of Wisconsin names it the Mineral Point branch of the Pecatonica. Two 1908 Wisconsin Geological and Natural History Survey maps have it labeled as Mineral Point Creek, and a circa 1911 postcard calls it Zinc Furnace Creek. That name most certainly relates to the Merry Christmas Mine zinc concentrating mill which was located on the banks of Mineral Point Creek a short distance upstream from where the photo was taken.

Left: Postcard of Zinc Furnace Creek. Mineral Point Library Archives. Right: Merry Christmas Mine zinc concentrating mill on the banks of Mineral Point Creek. Mineral Point Library Archives.

The "2008 Wisconsin Atlas & Gazetteer" and the "2007 Iowa County Land Atlas" now call it Brewery Creek. When the stream, whatever name you choose to call it, joins downstream with the Rock Branch and flows on towards the Pecatonica, it is known as Furnace Creek.

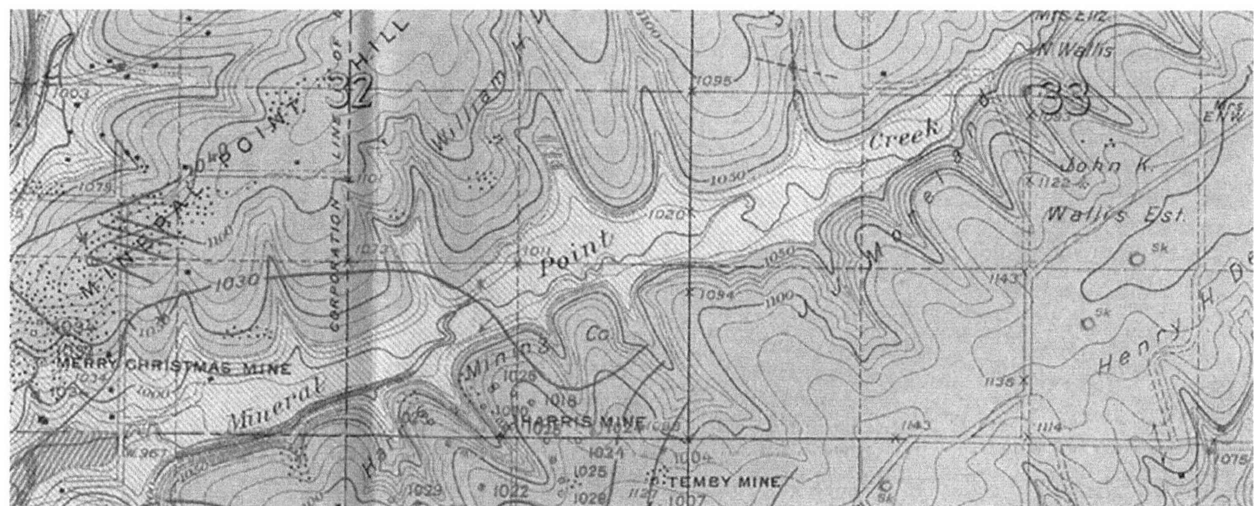

The above 1908 Wisconsin Geological and Natural History Survey map shows Mineral Point Hill on the left and Mineral Point Creek as it winds its way southwest towards Mineral Point.

The 1908 Wisconsin Geological and Natural History Survey map below shows Darlington Road heading east between two bluffs. "Mineral Point Hill" runs northeast of the railroad depot. These rocky bluffs are the gateway to the Darlington Road valley.

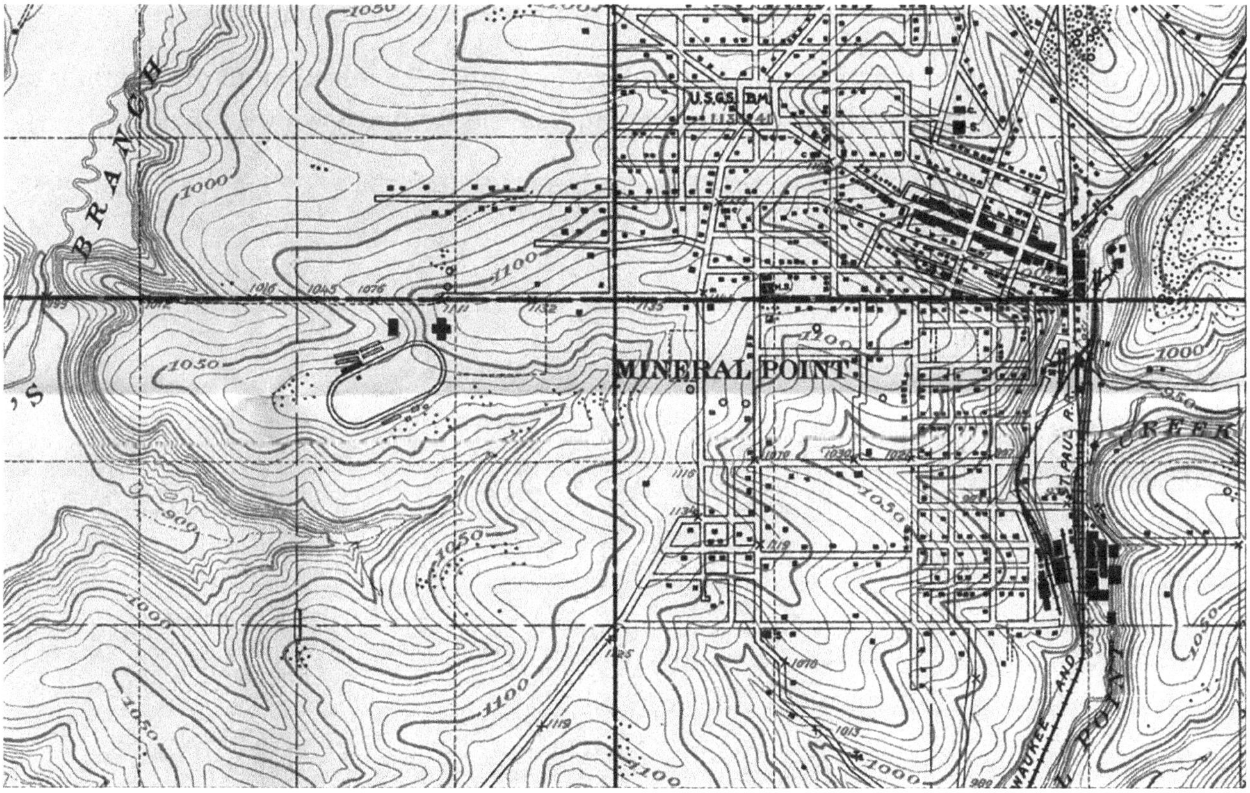

John Sharp 2019

The bluff at the south end of "Mineral Point Hill" can be seen east of the railroad depot in this photo. As Darlington Road leaves the city, it rounds this "Rocky Point" of the Mineral Point Hill and works its way up the valley, crossing Mineral Point Creek and continuing on a short distance to where it forks and goes north on Dodge Street or south towards Darlington.

The land surface for the first half mile up Darlington Road valley is a mix of bluffs and foothills on either side, with the Mineral Point Creek meandering from side to side down the middle.

The hills on the north side of the creek and road had very little commercial development. It was mainly a grassy hillside peppered with badger holes along the top of Mineral Point Hill. In later years there were a few small homes, and it remained mostly grazing land.

The southern "Rocky Point" and bluff of Mineral Point Hill. John Sharp 2019

Small homes on the north side of Darlington Road, circa 1900. Mineral Point Library Archives

Mineral Point Creek on the south side of the road presented a very different and attractive situation to early entrepreneurs. The valley was flat, and the stream's year-round potential for generating water power attracted several businesses, including the Mineral Point City Mill—1845, the Mineral Point Woolen Mill—1890 and the Badger Rubber Works—1906. Those businesses would be built at the entrance to the Darlington Road valley on Mineral Point Creek.

Other businesses built along the creek were the Vivian/Musgrove Lead Furnaces—1839, Whitney Smith Tannery—1860, John Hadfield Tallow Factory—1883 and the Mineral Point Construction Company—1909.

CHAPTER 3: MERRY CHRISTMAS MINE BUILDING, 1836–PRESENT

Merry Christmas Mine building circa 1940. Mineral Point Library Archives

This beautiful stone building that sits on the eastern slope of the Mineral Point Hill within Mineral Point has a history that begins in the earliest days of the city. It, along with other parcels of land on Merry Christmas Hill, was purchased by the State of Wisconsin in 1971. The building is now part of the Pendarvis Historic Site. When was this "good rock house" built, who built it and what is its history? Hopefully the following historical documents and other clues will help answer some of these questions.

Prior to the construction of the new Highway 39/23 bypass in 1948, and 1/2 mile east of the Mineral Point Railroad Depot, Darlington Road forked near the old town hall site. The main Darlington Road track continued up and around the hill to the south on its way toward the town of Darlington. The lesser traveled left-hand fork dropped off the hillside and turned north on Dodge Street, now known as Merry Christmas Lane. A short distance up Merry Christmas Lane and across Mineral Point Creek, the Merry Christmas Mine building is located on the west side of the road. This location is described as the south half of outlot 224 in Harrison's Survey of the City of Mineral Point.

The south half of outlot 224 was one of the earliest lots in Mineral Point to be developed and granted a preemption certificate. These certificates gave miners or settlers who developed land prior to 1834 "squatter's rights," which entitled them first rights to purchase the land they had developed at a minimum price. Final purchase of the land from the federal government was executed at a later date with a land patent.

Outlots 223, 224, 226, 227, 228 and 229 of Harrison's Survey, City of Mineral Point were some of the first lands developed in the mining district of Mineral Point. Preemption certificates on these outlots were filed July 5th, 1839, by Francis Vivian. (United States of America to Francis Vivian, abstract entry August 12, 1839.)

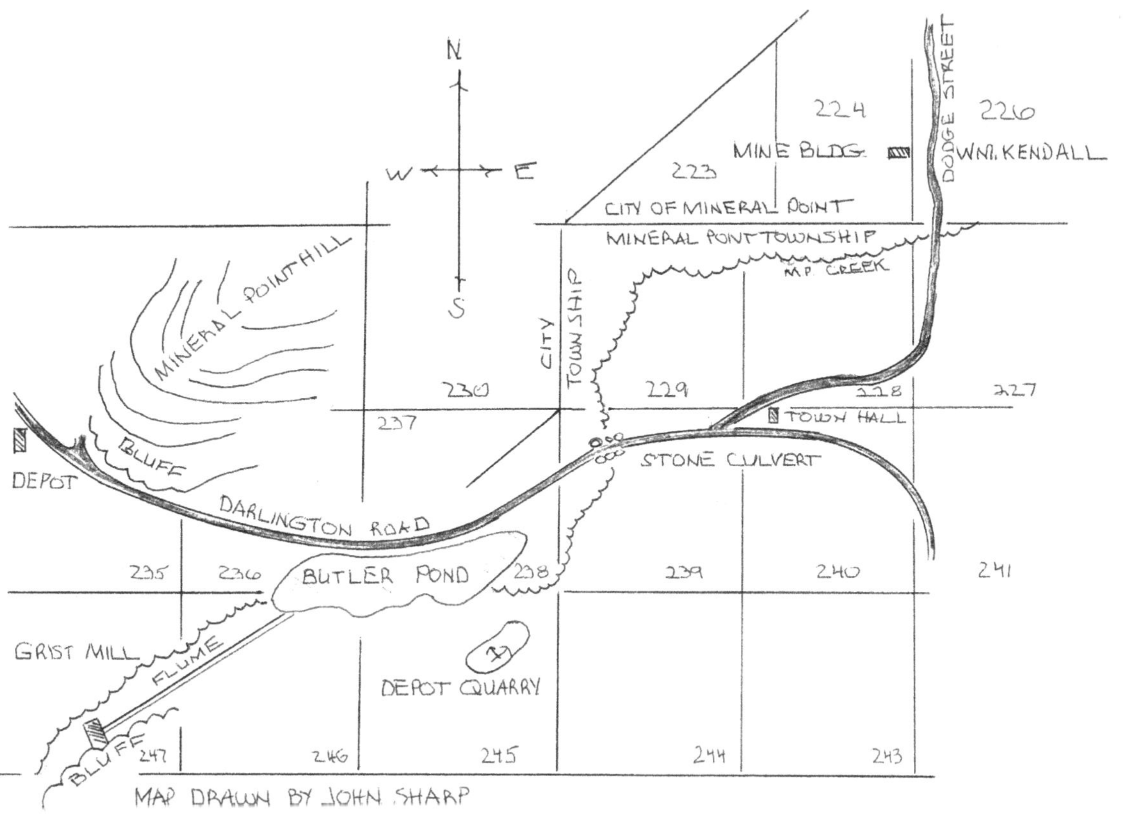

Francis Vivian was a tin and copper miner who immigrated from Camborne, Cornwall, England, to the United States and Mineral Point in 1832. The "1881 History of Iowa County" says that soon after his arrival to Mineral Point, he participated in the Black Hawk War. When the war ended, Mr. Vivian mined lead for a year on the Van Meter survey north of Mineral Point. He then spent a few months in Dubuque, Iowa, eventually returning to Mineral Point where he kept a store and partnered with Jacob Jenkins & John Musgrove in the smelting business.

Six months after Francis Vivian filed preemption certificates on outlots 223, 224, 226, 227, 228 and 229, he sold outlots 223, 224, 228 and 229 by warranty deed to his partners, John Musgrove and Jacob Jenkins. The sale deeds to Musgrove and Jenkins were recorded as follows:

On January 4, 1840, Francis Vivian sold an undivided 1/3 of outlots 223, 224, 228 and 229 by warranty deed to John Musgrove (with other lands). Recorded March 11, 1840, Vol. H Deeds, page 292.

On January 4, 1840, Francis Vivian sold an undivided 2/3 of outlots 223, 224, 228 and 229 by warranty deed to Jacob Jenkins (with other lands). Recorded October 22, 1840, Vol. H Deeds, page 491.

Of the four outlots Francis Vivian sold to his partners, only outlots **224** and **228** are of interest in this chapter. Outlot 224 is most significant since it is on the south half of this outlot that the Merry Christmas Mine building is located.

The preemption certificates Francis Vivian applied for on outlots 224 and 228 record early valuable and historical information about these two outlots by documenting improvements that had been made to the land prior to 1836. 1836 is a very early date in Mineral Point history. It is only two years after the government land office was opened in Mineral Point and nine years after the discovery of lead on Mineral Point Hill in 1827.

The preemption certificate on outlot 224 states the lot was improved by a **"building"** previous to 1836. The preemption certificate on outlot 228 states the lot was improved by **"enclosures"** previous to 1836. This information will prove to be significant. These same improvements had to have been on the land four months later when Vivian sold outlots 224 and 228 to his partners, Jacob Jenkins and John Musgrove.

The preemption certificate on outlot 224 reads as follows:

To the commissioners appointed to lay off the towns of Mineral (Point) etc.

I apply for certificate of preemption for lot No. 224 in Mineral Point, and in support of my claim, offer testimony.

Francis Vivian assignee of John Doherty, Henry Carter, John Price & John Dill

Wm. Kendal being sworn on his oath says that he is acquainted with lot No. 224 in Mineral Point, that it was improved by ***building*** *previous to the 2nd of July 1836, that it is in peaceable possession of the applicant, and that the deponent has no claim to said lot.*

Subscribed and Warrents before us on July 5, 1839 *Wm. Kendall*

George Cubbage

William Corvile

The preemption certificate on outlot 228 reads as follows:

To the commissioners appointed to lay off the towns of Mineral Point etc.

I apply for certificate of preemption for lot No. 228 in Mineral Point and in support of my claim offer testimony.

Francis Vivian assignee of John Bostwick, James Davis, Jacob Stout & Manlove Hays

Wm. Kendall being sworn on his oath says that he is acquainted with lot No 228 in Mineral Point, that It was improved by ***enclosures*** *previous to the 2nd of July, 1836, that it is in the peaceable possession of the claimant, and that the deponent has no claim to said lot.*

Subscribed and sworn to before us on July 5, 1839 *Wm. Kendall*

George Cubbage

Willam Corvile

On March 22, 1839, an important and historically significant advertisement appeared in the Mineral Point *Miners Free Press* newspaper. Although this ad does not refer to a specific location, many of the items listed for sale can be linked to outlots 224 and 228, including the Merry Christmas Mine building. The ad was titled "Valuable Furnace for Sale."

Miners Free Press, March 22, 1839

VALUABLE FURNACE FOR SALE

For sale one-third of the very valuable Lead Furnace situated within the corporation of Mineral Point, and now belonging to Jacob Jenkin & Co. That part of the property now offered for sale comprises one-third of 30 acres of town land, on which the furnace now stands, two furnaces quite new and in thorough repair, a Lime Kiln with 750 bushels of Lime, a good Coal Shed which will contain 6,000 bushels, three good Cabins, and logs for two more, extensive Stabbling, (stabling) and an acre of Garden, nine Oxen, two Milch Cows, Wagon, mineral and Sleigh, good root House and Cellar, &c. It has a stream calculated for any weight of machinery at any time of year, and it is worthy of notice that the severest weather does not put a stop to the operation. To be sold also with the same, one-half of a crushing machine, in a good rock house adjoining the Furnace, with Washing Utensils, &c., complete.

The above premises are a good investment for capital and deserving the immediate attention of speculators or others. They are in the mining district, and the situation is such that procuring of mineral is attended with less expense than that of any other furnace in the neighborhood. They are offered for sale forthwith, and further particulars may be obtained by applying to John Musgrove, the present proprietors on the premises, or Garry and Rosewarnes, Corner of Commerce and Fountain Streets Mineral Point.

March 22, 1839

This ad, Like Francis Vivian's preemption certificates, records early and valuable historical information. It advertises a compound of several structures and a stream, all situated within the corporation of Mineral Point. The size and number of the structures listed in this ad were substantial and would have taken months if not years to build. The structures included two furnaces, a good rock house, a root cellar, three good log cabins, a coal shed and extensive "Stabbling." Obviously these improvements existed before the ad was placed in 1839, and even before Francis Vivian filed his preemption certificates in 1839, and the date of the ad is less than four months before Vivian sold outlot 224 and 228 to his partners, Jacob Jenkins and John Musgrove on July 4, 1840.

Francis Vivian was the owner of outlots 224 and 228 when the ad was placed March 22, 1839. Jacob Jenkins and John Musgrove were listed as owner and proprietor respectively of the "very valuable Lead Furnace adjoining a good rock house" in the 1839 ad. In addition to being named as owner and proprietor of a "very valuable Lead Furnace adjoining a good rock house," Francis Vivian's partners became the official owners of outlots 224 and 228 soon after the ad was published. The

Merry Christmas Mine building is "a good rock house" located on outlot 224, land owned by Jacob Jenkins and John Musgrove. The three partners, Francis Vivian, Jacob Jenkins and John Musgrove, bought and sold outlots 223, 224, 228 and 229 back and forth to one another until John and Nancy Musgrove ultimately sold the lots to Alexander C Davis in 1851. (Warranty Deed. January 7, 1851, Vol. Q Deeds, page 108. Consideration $6,153.20.)

It seems as though Francis Vivian, Jacob Jenkins and John Musgrove were doing some wheeling and dealing with this land and the compound of structures.

William Kendall, a Cornish companion of Francis Vivian, swore in Vivian's preemption certificate on outlot 224 that the lot had been improved by a ***building*** prior to 1836. Was the "building" mentioned in the preemption certificate on outlot 224 the same "good rock house" that was advertised for sale in the 1839 *Miners Free Press*? If so, then the rock house listed in the ad corroborates William Kendall's testimony that outlot 224 was improved by a "building."

Another clue that links the ad to this land is a ***stream***. The ad advertises a stream "at any time of year." The only stream on outlot 224 or 228 is Mineral Point Creek, which runs through outlot 228. This stream has a good flow "at any time of year," and it is only a stone's throw from the Merry Christmas Mine building.

The parallels between Francis Vivian, Jacob Jenkins, John Musgrove, "a good rock house," "a valuable furnace" and the stream are striking. They all seem to converge in the year 1839 on outlots 224 and 228.

Additional documents will connect outlots 224 and 228 to the 1839 *Miners Free Press* ad and the Merry Christmas Mine building, all located "within the corporation of Mineral Point" as mentioned in the ad.

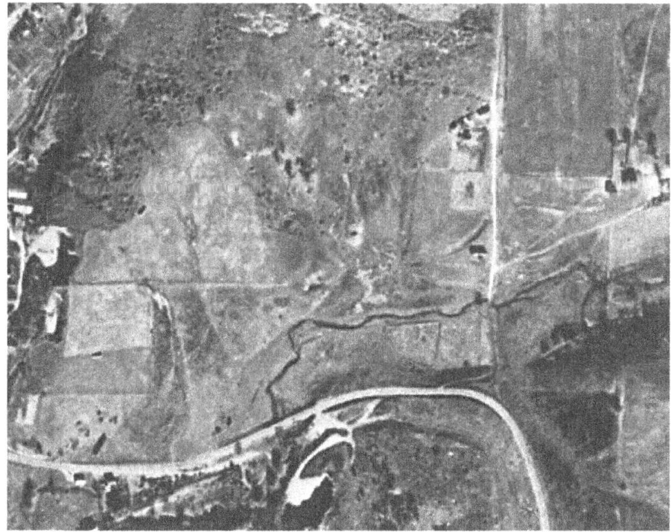

1937 Wisconsin Department of Transportation Aerial Photograph

This October 30, 1937 Wisconsin Department of Transportation aerial photograph reveals physical evidence that links items listed in the ad to outlot 224. Forty feet south and running west of the Merry Christmas Mine building on outlots 224, the faint, white ghost shadow of a large rock foundation can be seen. These partially buried rock foundations around Mineral Point tend to show themselves when the soil dries out and the shallow rooted grasses growing over them turn brown. Because of its rectangular shape and large size, approximately 72 x 144, this ghost-shadow foundation is most likely revealing where a large lead furnace once stood, adjoining the Merry Christmas Mine building. The location of the furnace foundation in this aerial was only forty feet from the Merry Christmas Mine building, "a good rock house." If the rock foundation was a lead furnace, it corresponds perfectly with the wording of "a good rock house adjoining the Furnace" in the ad and suggests the advertisement is referring to the Merry Christmas Mine building and this hidden rock foundation on outlot 224.

This 1937 aerial also confirms the ad's listing of a stream "at any time of year." Mineral Point Creek just below the Merry Christmas Mine building runs year-round from east to west through outlot 228. It is the only stream located on outlots 224 or 228 and is most likely the stream referred to in the 1839 ad as a stream "at any time of year."

William Kendall also swore in Francis Vivian's 1839 preemption certificate on outlot 228 that the land was improved by ***"enclosures"*** prior to 1836. The rich bottom land south of Mineral Point Creek over to the Darlington Road hillside could have had multiple "enclosures," one for "an acre of Garden" and one for "nine Oxen and two Milch Cows" as listed in the 1839 *Miners Free Press* ad. The dark straight lines south of the creek in this 1937 DOT aerial indicates that this fertile bottom land has been used for gardening or for keeping livestock in more recent times. It would make sense to place "enclosures" where there was good grass and running water.

The 1836/1844 Mineral Point and Environs Map shows Vivian's Furnace located along the north bank of Mineral Point Creek on outlot 228. This sliver of land is solid dry ground and is directly south of where the Merry Christmas Mine building and the ghost-shadow furnace foundation are located on outlot 224.

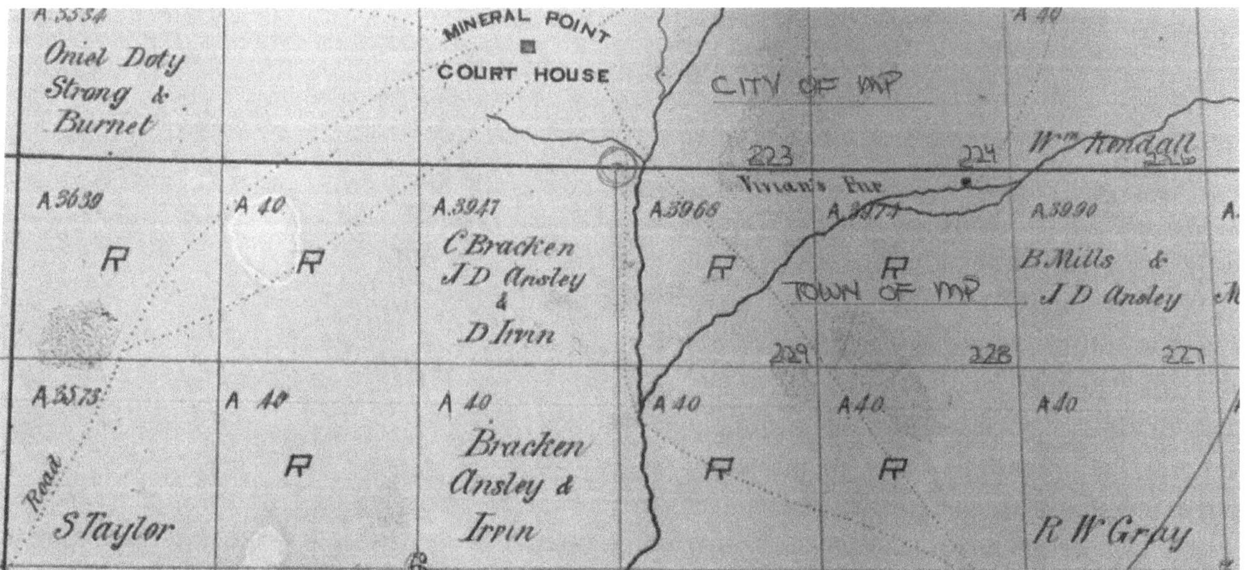

1836/1844 Mineral Point and Environs Map. Mineral Point Library Archives

The *Miners Free Press* advertisement lists "two furnaces quite new and in thorough repair" for sale. Is it possible the advertisement is referring to Vivian's Furnace on outlot 228 and a furnace whose large rock foundation has been revealed on outlot 224? The actual relationship between the Vivian Furnace as shown on the Mineral Point and Environs map and the ghost-shadow foundation of a furnace adjoining the Merry Christmas Mine building on outlot 224 seems to authenticate descriptions given in the advertisement.

Another clue and early bit of historical information that authenticates information advertised in the 1839 *Miners Free Press* ad is found in a journal entry that appears in the autobiography of William Lewis Manly. Manly was a pioneer adventurer from Michigan who traveled west into Wisconsin with a friend in the 1840s. In his autobiography, "Death Valley in '49," he wrote an interesting account of crossing the Wisconsin prairies toward Mineral Point and working at Vivian's smelting furnace.

LOUIS MANLY'S JOURNAL 1840

...we set out across the prairie toward Mineral Point, twenty miles away. When within four miles of that place we stopped at the house of Daniel Parkinson, a fine-looking two-story building, and after a meal was over, Mr. Henry (Manly's friend) hired out to him for $16 per month and went to work that day... I now went to Mineral Point and searched the town over for work. My purse contained thirty-five cents only, and I slept in an unoccupied outhouse without supper. I bought crackers and dried beef for ten cents in the morning and made my first meal since the day before, felt pretty low-spirited. I then went to **Vivian's smelting furnace** where they bought lead ore, smelted it and run it into pigs of about 70 pounds each. He said he had a job for me if I could do it. The furnace was **propelled by water**, and they had a small buzz saw for cutting four-foot wood into blocks about a foot long. These blocks they wanted split up in pieces about an inch square to mix in with charcoal in smelting ore. He said he would board me with the other men and give me a dollar and a quarter a cord for splitting wood. I felt awfully poor, and a stranger, and this was a beginning for me at any rate, so I went to work with a will and never lost a minute of daylight till I had split up all the wood and filled his woodhouse completely up. The board was very coarse—bacon, potatoes and bread—a man cook and bread mixed up with salt water. The **log house** where we lodged was well infested with troublesome insects which worked nights at any rate, whether they rested days or not, and the beds had a mild odor of pole cat. The house was long, low and without windows. In one end was a fireplace, and there were two tiers of bunks on each side, supplied with straw only. In the space between the bunks was a stationary table with stools for seats. I was the only American who boarded there, and I could not well become very familiar with the boarders...

Louise Manly's account of being boarded in a log house and Vivian's Furnace being propelled by water gives actual on-the-ground verification and support to the 1839 *Miners Free Press* ad listing "three good cabins with logs for two more" and "a stream at any time of year."

Vivian's smelting furnace on outlot 228 was very near the large rock foundation of a furnace revealed on outlot 224 by the aerial photo. These **two furnaces** and the adjoining **good rock house** were part of a compound of structures that match those advertised in the 1839 *Miners Free Press* ad. Manly's reference to Vivian's Furnace being propelled by water power would require a stream **"any time of year"** as advertised, and the old **log house** where Manly lodged corroborates with the log cabins listed for sale in the 1839 *Miners Free Press* ad.

The most significant items listed in the 1839 *Miners Free Press* advertisement are "a good rock house" and "the very valuable lead furnace." The Merry Christmas Mine building adjoining the furnace foundation on outlot 224 corresponds with what the *Miners Free Press* is advertising and places these two items as part of a larger compound of structures that are located on outlots 224 and 228.

Jacob Jenkins and John Musgrove were named in the ad as owner and proprietor respectively of "the very valuable Lead Furnace" adjoining "the good rock house." This seems to be good, solid evidence that these men, the two furnaces, the rock house on outlot 224, the log cabins and Vivian's water-powered furnace mentioned in Manly's autobiography can all be linked to the compound of items listed in the 1839 *Miners Free Press* ad. These facts and others included in the ad appear to be talking about a compound of structures located on outlots 224 and 228, all "within the corporation of Mineral Point."

These facts and clues also indicate that either Francis Vivian, John Musgove or Jacob Jenkins built the Merry Christmas Mine building in the middle 1830s. Since exact proof has not been discovered as of yet, the strong correlations between the ad, the known facts on the ground and an abundance of circumstantial evidence bring me to conclude that John Musgrove built or had someone build the Merry Christmas Mine building, and it was indeed constructed in the middle 1830s. The following Mineral Point newspaper articles lend support that the Merry Christmas Mine building was built by John Musgrove, since it was known as the "Musgrove furnace/place/house" up until 1906, when the Merry Christmas Mine was opened.

Early References to Musgrove Include:

May 6, 1846

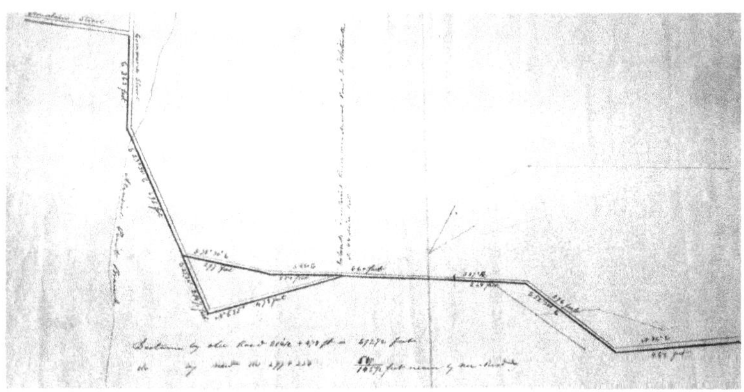

1846 survey map. Mineral Point Library Archives

On May 6, 1846, the Mineral Point Corporation had a "Survey of an alteration in the 'Road' between Lanyon Blacksmith Shop and John Musgrove Furnace." This alteration shortened the "Road" (Darlington Road) between these two establishments by 145-1/2 feet.

The Lanyon Blacksmith Shop was located on Commerce Street, and the Musgrove Furnace was located near the Merry Christmas Mine building.

Wisconsin Tribune, September 22, 1853

THREE MEN SHOT

On Saturday afternoon last, at a shooting match near **Musgrove's** Furnace, in this town, three men were shot through the legs by the discharge of a gun thrown violently upon the ground by a man in a state of intoxication. There appeared to have been some slight misunderstanding, which threw the man into a rage, whereupon he threw his gun with such force as to break the stock, and cause the discharge.

Mineral Point Tribune, March 30, 1854

...We learn, also, that this company (Mississippi Mining and Manufacturing Co.) has purchased the furnace known as the **Musgrove** Furnace and intend to put it in operations immediately...

Mineral Point Weekly Tribune, July 2, 1861

NEW LIME KILN AT *MUSGROVE'S* FURNACE

This *Tribune* ad lends support to the existence of the lime kiln at **Musgrove's** Furnace as listed in the 1839 *Miners Free Press* ad.

Mineral Point Weekly Tribune, May 29, 1867

...Winnebagos who make their annual visits about this time of year. Their camp was near **Musgrove's** old furnace...

On April 18, 1881, Philip Allen Sr. purchased the south half of outlot 224 and the north half of outlot 228. (April 18, 1881, Warranty Deed, Vol. 37 Deeds, page 219. Consideration $400).

Iowa County Democrat, June 5, 1885

COUNCIL PROCEEDINGS

Mr. Joseph Bennett, overseer of road district No. 5, of the town of Mineral Point, was present and requested assistance from the city in building a new bridge in his district near the old **Musgrove** house...

Mineral Point Tribune, May 7, 1886

The application of Mr. Joseph Bennett for assistance in building a bridge near the old **Musgrove** place in the town of Mineral Point was referred to Alderman Snow, Varcoe and Allen.

Over the next several years, outlots 223, 224, 228, and 229, along with other lands, were bought and sold to several entities. The Merry Christmas Mine was opened January of 1906, when Phillip Allen Sr. owned the south outlot 224 and the north outlot 228.

Mineral Point Tribune, January 4, 1906

The Merry Christmas Mine, opened up on the Mineral Point Hill by Ike Suthers and others, is proving a dandy, and the owners have refused $15,000 for it.

Iowa County Democrat, August 29, 1907

THE MINERAL POINT HILL AGAIN THE SEENE (SCENE) OF ACTIVE MINING OPERATIONS
A CONCENTRATING MILL
BUILDING ON THE STREAM NEAR THE TOWN HALL

Not since the days of the old **Musgrove lead furnace** has the Mineral Point Hill witnessed such great activity in industrial operations as during the fall season of 1907. The Merry Christmas company has purchased several tracts of ground from W. P. Gundry, Spensly & McIlhon, P. Whalen and others, and are preparing to push their mining and milling operation on a large scale. They are tunneling the hill from the south and will run their ores down to a point a short distance north of the town hall, where they are erecting a large concentrating mill.

The **large stone house** which stands at the foot of the hill, and which has been unoccupied for a long time, is being repaired and fitted up for occupancy by employees of the mining company.

The valley and hillsides above old Butler's dam certainly promises to take on new life and activity. A short distance east and further up the stream are the Harris and Temby mines, which are to be operated on a very extensive scale.

The naming of the "Musgrove lead furnace" in this article is probably one of the last references to Musgrove. The long unoccupied large stone house (Merry Christmas Mine building) at the foot of the hill was repaired for employees of the mining company. It was probably around this time when people began referring to the Musgrove house as the Merry Christmas Mine building.

Iowa County Democrat, September 12, 1907

The Merry Christmas is driving a tunnel into the old "Mineral Point Hill." The foundations for the new mill have been completed, and the superstructure is being reared by a large force of competent mechanics in the employ of the Galena Iron Works company.

In 1908, the heirs of Philip Allen Sr. sold the south half of outlot 224 and the north half of outlot 228 to George Ehrat and William Molard, Chicago cheese merchants. (March 27, 1908, Warranty Deed, Vol. 80 Deeds, page 137. Consideration $800.00.)

Iowa County Democrat, May 14, 1908

AND STILL IT IS MINERAL POINT HILL

The longevity and permanency of Mineral Point as a prosperous mining town is fully established by the fact that the Mineral Point Hill, where over eighty years ago (1828,) lead ore was found in great abundance, is now yielding abundantly of rich lead and zinc ores. The output at the Merry Christmas Mine, which is located on the famous old Mineral Point Hill, tells its own strong story of the wealth underneath. The miners have uncovered a great sheet of black jack and lead, which promises well for the Merry Christmas.

Mineral Point Tribune, March 25, 1909

Geo. Ehrat of Chicago was in our city last Friday and made arrangements with Geo. S. Huxtable to dispose of the mining equipment of the Merry Christmas Mine. Persons contemplating the purchase of machinery of this kind would do well to correspond or come to investigate.

Mineral Point Tribune, July 15, 1909

The Merry Christmas Mining Company of this city has sublet its entire leasehold and equipment to Stude & Co., local operators, who have opened the ground in new quarters, striking big chunk lead, in some instances, cogs being hoisted to the surface weighing 500 pounds each.

Mineral Point Tribune, May 4, 1911

The Merry Christmas Mining Company is shut down, and reports are that negotiations are on foot for the sale of the mine, land and equipment. The property is owned by wholesale cheese merchants of Chicago, (George Ehar & William Molard), who purchased fee to the 45 acres of land and equipment with a plant involving an outlay of about $20,000. The mine made a very good showing last season.

The Mineral Point Zinc Company purchased this land from Ehrat and Molard on January 16, 1912.

Iowa County Democrat, October 19, 1911

SALE OF A LOCAL MINE

THE MERRY CHRISTMAS BOUGHT BY THE MINERAL POINT ZINC COMPANY

> The Merry Christmas Mine, which is in the city limits, a short distance east of the railway station, has been sold by Messers,. Ehrat and Molard to the Mineral Point Zinc Company. The new owners will further develop the property in their customary thorough manner, and there will again be something doing in the interior of the old Mineral Point Hill, where extensive mining operations were carried on over 80 years ago. (Molard and Ehrat to Mineral Point Zinc Company, Quit Claim Deed, January 16, 1912, Vol. 88 Deeds, page 1. Consideration $9,000.00.)

Mineral Point Tribune, May 30, 1912

> The Merry Christmas Mine, now owned by the New Jersey Zinc Company, has remained closed since passing into control of the zinc corporation.

Mineral Point Tribune, October 3, 1912

> The Merry Christmas Mine, which passed into the ownership and control of the New Jersey Zinc Company, has resumed operations.

On December 13, 1937, the Mineral Point Zinc Company sold the south half of outlot 224 and the north of outlot 228, along with other parcels, to the Empire Zinc Company for $38,461.47, and on April 1, 1943, the Empire Zinc Company sold these same lots along with other parcels to Leo and Agnes Gillmann.

On January 7, 1951, John and Nancy Musgrove sold outlots 223, 224, 228 and 229 in Mineral Point (with other lands) to Alexander Davis, and the Merry Christmas Mine building continued to be referred to as the "old Musgrove house."

On December 28, 1971, the widow Agnes Gillmann sold the Merry Christmas Mine hill to the State of Wisconsin and the State Historical Society of Wisconsin for $38,000.00. (Land Contract, December 28, 1971, Vol. 275, page 388.)

Merry Christmas Mine Building, "a good rock house," 1839–2023.
John Sharp 2021

CHAPTER 4: MINERAL POINT CITY MILL, 1849-1890

The Mineral Point City Mill was built between 1845 and 1849 and was the first flour mill in Mineral Point and the first business to locate along Mineral Point Creek and Darlington Road. Even though a grist mill in town was of exceptional importance to farmers and citizens, the Mineral Point City Mill did not become operational until 1857. Farmers had to travel great distances by horse and wagon to get their grain to a mill for grinding.

Matilda Hood, who was one of Mineral Point's earliest settlers, gained title by land patent to several lots along Mineral Point Creek and Darlington Road starting in 1837. She and her husband, John, came to Mineral Point from Missouri in 1828. Matilda lived in Mineral Point until her death in 1879, and she was involved in various business ventures during her time in "Point."

Because of the need for a facility to grind grain in or near Mineral Point, and because Matilda owned land on Mineral Point Creek, she and a man named Benjamin Butler entered into a partnership agreement in 1845 to build a grist mill on part of outlot 247, owned by Matilda and located on the creek. Water from the creek would be used to turn the mill stones to grind wheat into bolted flour. Hood and Butler reached their agreement on the third day of March, 1845.

The first portion of this agreement reads as follows:

> This Indenture made the third day of March in the year of our Lord one thousand eight hundred and forty five between Matilda E. Hood of the County of Iowa and Territory of Wisconsin of the first part and Benjamin Butler of the County and Territory of the Second part witnesseth that this said party of the first part for and in consideration of the sum of five hundred dollars lawful money of the United States to her in hand paid by the said party of the second part the receipt whereof or hereby conferred and acknowledged have given, granted, bargained, sold, surmised, released, aligned and confirmed, and by these presents do give, garnish, bargain, sell, surmise, release, align and confirm unto the said party of the second part and to his heirs and assigns forever the undivided half part share of the following described land and mill privilege situate lying and being in the Town of Mineral Point, County of Iowa and Territory of Wisconsin and is known and distinguished on the map of survey of said town into lots as part of outlot number two hundred forty seven (247) beginning at the southwest corner of said lot thence east three hundred & thirty feet thence north one hundred & sixty five feet thence south seventy eight degrees west thence three hundred thirty six feet thence ninety nine feet to the place of beginning with the privilege of making and keeping in repair a head race from the east line of the above described land across said Lot No. 247, and into about the middle of Lot No. 246. and then to build erect and keep in repair a mill dam and also the privilege of making and keeping in repair a road across said mill dam and along the east embankment of the head race and also the privilege

> of floating with water what land it may become necessary to flow for the benefit of the mill on the remainder of Lot No. 246, and on outlots 245, 244, 239, & 238.

When Matilda Hood and Benjamin Butler agreed to build a grist mill in March 1845, Butler signed a $500 mortgage with Matilda, giving him an undivided half share of the land on outlot 247 where the mill would be located, along with mill privileges. Butler was also given the privilege of water from her land to fill a mill pond for the benefit of the mill. In return, Butler was to get a grist mill up and running by building a mill dam, head race, road across the dam to access the mill and presumably a mill building, although no mill building was mentioned in the 1845 agreement. Matilda expected to become half owner of the mill and its profits.

Over the next four years, Butler worked at developing the mill particulars that he and Matilda had agreed upon. He constructed the agreed-upon mill dam, which became known as the "Butler Pond," built the road over the dam and along the mill race to access the mill, and as was stated in a law suit filed by Matilda against Butler in 1851, she and Butler had mutually agreed to share the expense of building the grist mill building, which they did. Butler was also expected to manage the building of the mill, which he did, and put it into service.

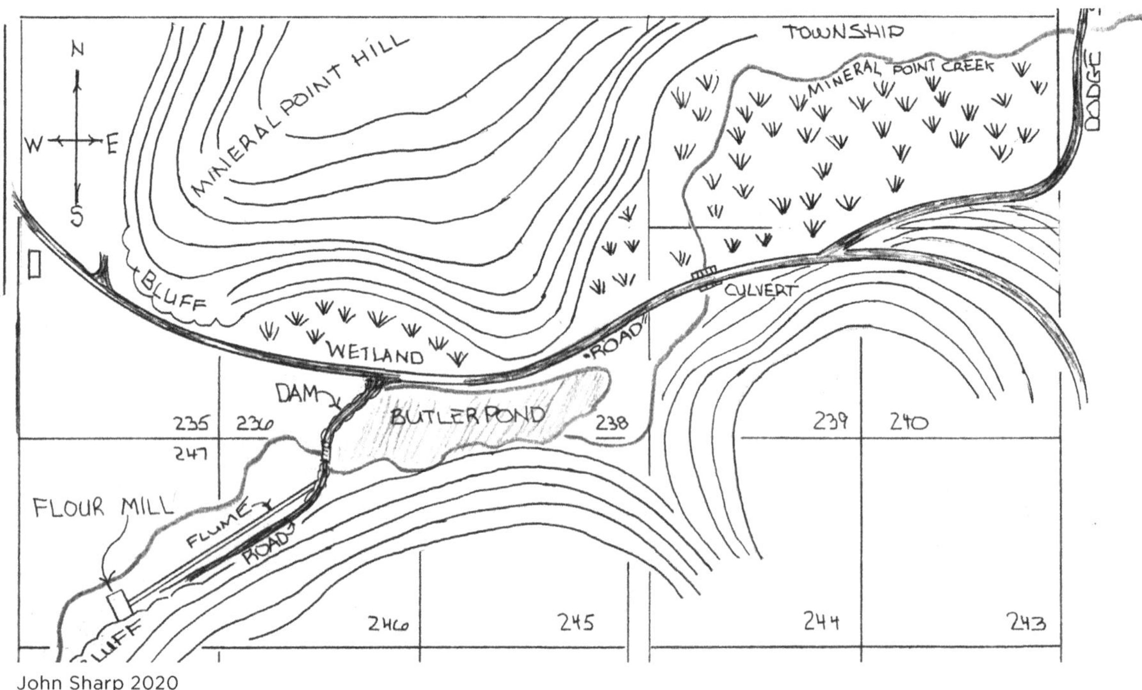

John Sharp 2020

As an aside, it is interesting to note that after the Hood/Butler agreement in 1845, the territory of Wisconsin became the 30th state in the union on May 29, 1848.

On the 14th day of November, 1849, for some unknown reason and to the *"great frustration"* of Matilda, Butler sold his half share of the mill and its improvements to Thomas Davey for $200 and left town for *"Parts unknown."* Butler had not finished the mill and put it into operation, and he had not paid off his mortgage to Matilda. Butler was able to sell his interest in the mill by deed to Davey more or less legally since Matilda had neglected to have her mortgage with Butler recorded, and the mortgage was by some means unknown to her lost and came into the hands and possession of Butler and Davey.

The agreement between Butler and Davey reads as follows:

> Benjamin Butler To Thomas Davey
>
> Received November 14, 1849 at 12 o'clock Meridian
>
> Know all men by these presents that I, Benjamin Butler of the Town of Mineral Point in the County of Iowa and State of Wisconsin, in consideration of Two Hundred Dollars paid by Thomas Davey of same place, the recelpt which is hereby acknowledged. Do hereby give grant bargain, sell and convey unto the said Thomas Davey, the following described real estate to wit. The equal undivided half part of Lot Number two hundred and forty-seven (247). The same being an out lot which is bounded as follows beginning at the Southwest corner of said lot. Thence east three hundred and thirty feet, thence north one hundred and sixth five feet thence south seventy eight degrees west three hundred and thirty six feet, thence ninety nine feet to the place of beginning, with the privilege of making and keeping in repair a head race from the east line of the above described land thereof, said lot No. two hundred & forty seven (247) and into about the middle of lot no. two hundred and forty six (246) and then to make and to keep in repair a mill dam and also the privilege of making & keeping in repair a road across said mill dam, and along the embankment of said head race, and also the privilege of floating with water what land it may become necessary to flow for the benefit of the mill the remainder of out Lot No. Two Hundred and Forty Six & out Lot Two Hundred and Forty Four, Two Hundred and Forty Five, Two Hundred and Thirty Eight and Two Hundred and Thirty Nine all the lots above described being out lots in the Town of Mineral Point aforesaid and the property above enjoyned, being the same, as conveyed to me by Matilda Hood, the third day of March 1845. To have and to hold the above granted premises to the said Thomas Davey his heirs and assigns to their use and belong forever.
>
> And I the said Benjamin Butler for myself and my heirs executors and administrators, Do covenant with the said Thomas Davey his heirs and assigns, that I am lawfully slgned In fee simple of the afore granted premises, that they are free from all incumbencies. That I have good right to sell and convey the same, to said Thomas Davey his heirs and assigns forever as aforesaid, and that I will and my heirs, executors and administrators shall warrant and defend the same to the said Thomas Davey his heirs and assigns forever against the lawful claims and demands of all persons.
>
> In witness where of I the said Benjamin Butler have herewith set my hand and seal this thirteenth day of October in the year of our Lord eighteen hundred and forty nine.

Needless to say, the property was not free from incumbencies as the sale document stated, since Butler had not paid off his mortgage to Hood.

So what happened to Benjamin Butler and his $200 after selling his share of the mill to Thomas Davey and disappearing to *"parts unknown?"* It is my theory, and only a theory, that Butler provisioned himself and headed west to the California gold fields. It's much more exciting to pan gold at Sutter's Mill than to grind wheat into flour at the Mineral Point City Mill. Mineral Point saw a huge drop in population when gold was discovered in California. Butler probably didn't see any future in milling flour with so many people leaving Mineral Point at a fever pitch. All businesses in town were paralyzed, and growing industries such as the flour mill would be crippled. Butler probably could see this and decided to leave town himself.

Matilda sued Butler and Thomas Davey on November 3, 1851, for the unpaid mortgage and the unethical transfer of property to Davey. Butler had to be sued in absentia since he had departed the area. The court found in favor of Hood, but Davey did not accept the decision and then sued Hood. The dispute was finally sent to arbitration, and the property was declared owned in common. Neither Davey nor Hood could agree or come to terms with this ruling, and the court ordered the property sold at auction. Notice of the sale was published for six weeks in the *Mineral Point Tribune*.

Mineral Point Tribune

I will, on Saturday, the tenth day of June A.D. 1854, between nine o'clock in the morning and the setting of the sun of said day to wit: at the hour of three o'clock p.m. of said day, at the front door of the Court House, in Mineral Point, in said county of Iowa, Wisconsin, offer for sale at public auction and sell to the highest bidder, all and singular the real estate in said decretal order.

C. N. Mumford
Sheriff, Iowa County, Wisconsin

The Mineral Point City Mill, in a run-down condition after several years of neglect and still not in operation, was purchased at the 1854 auction by Robert and William Lanyon for $1,150. The Lanyons had the mill for two years but did little to get it operational, and in 1856 sold their interests in the mill to Thomas Jenkins and John Roberts.

That same year, Jenkins procured a road easement from Matilda Hood across the dam and down the hillside along the water flume in order to access the mill. Jenkins and Roberts installed the needed machinery to mill wheat, introduced a steam engine for more power and finally got the Mineral Point City Mill operational.

Mineral Point Library Archives

Jenkins began milling wheat into flour in 1857 and produced a high-quality product for the next several years. During a heavy rain in 1866, the Butler Dam gave way, causing heavy damage downstream to the mill, railroad bridges and other businesses. Jenkins made the necessary repairs to the mill and continued operating the mill until 1867, at which time he sold the mill on contract to William Dawe for $4,850.

Dawe owned and operated the mill for eight years. In 1875, Dawe sold the mill on contract to George Orr and Norman Wright. Orr and Wright ended up selling the mill back to Mrs. Dawe, who had gained ownership in a divorce from her husband in 1876. Mrs. Dawe attempted to sell the mill in 1877 but could not. Later that year, she returned the mill to Thomas Jenkins, who held the original mortgage to William Dawe.

The Mineral Point City Mill continued its troubled history for the next 13 years. The mill and property had five different owners after the Dawes and was eventually acquired in 1890 by Phil Allen, who wanted the mill for the newly formed Mineral Point Woolen Mill.

One of the mill owners along the way was Sam Wright, who owned the mill from 1879 to 1886. In addition to operating the mill, Sam built a large ice house on Butler Dam where he could store large quantities of ice cut on the mill pond during the winter months to be sold the following summer.

A "personal brief" in the 1883 *Iowa County Democrat* reported that Sam Wright had men cutting ice on the Butler mill pond and storing it in his new ice house.

Iowa County Democrat, January 5, 1883

"Sam Wright has a large number of men engaged in filling his new and commodious ice house at his pond near the depot by one of the most ingenious labor contrivances we have seen. The ice is fifteen inches thick and of the finest quality."

This ad appeared in the August 4, 1882 *Iowa County Democrat*.

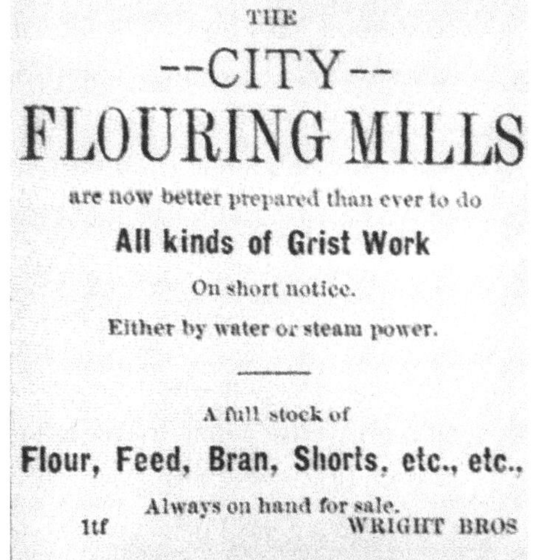

THE

--CITY--

FLOURING MILLS

are now better prepared than ever to do

All kinds of Grist Work

On short notice.

Either by water or steam power.

A full stock of

Flour, Feed, Bran, Shorts, etc., etc.,

Always on hand for sale.

1tf WRIGHT BROS

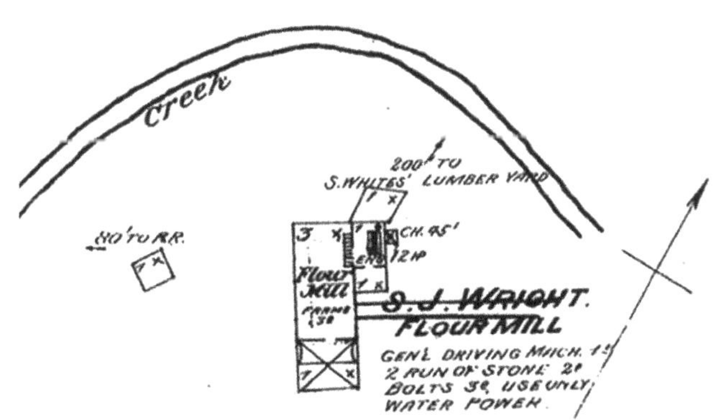

1884 Sanborn map shows the Sam Wright Flour Mill on Mineral Point Creek. Mineral Point Library Archives

Mineral Point Library Archives

In 1882, Butler Dam again suffered significant storm damage from heavy rains, putting the mill out of commission temporarily. Sam Wright, who owned the property at that time, had the dam and other damage repaired and continued to operate the mill and cut ice on the pond.

The ramp shown in this photo is probably the *"ingenious labor contrivance"* Wright used to push ice into the upper floors of his ice house.

In 1886, Wright sold his ice business and the mill to Thomas Sexton. After operating the businesses for one year, Sexton claimed that Wright had falsified his income records, and the businesses could not earn what he claimed. A lawsuit between the two owners ensued but could not be settled, and the mill was again sold at a sheriff's sale in 1889. A gentleman by the name of Matt Schmit purchased the mill and property at the sale for $505 on January 21, 1889.

On the 20th day of June, 1890, a torrential rain dumped millions of gallons of water on the Mineral Point Creek watershed and a *"Deluge of Great Magnitude"* came rushing down the valley and burst the Butler Dam for the third time in its history, sweeping everything before it and causing heavy damage to the mill and other properties as far as four miles downstream.

Iowa County Democrat, June 20, 1890

A VERY DESTRUCTIVE STORM.

MINERAL POINT VISITED BY A DELUGE OF GREAT MAGNITUDE.

BUTLER'S DAM BURSTS AND THE FLOOD SWEEPS EVERYTHING BEFORE IT.

THE DAMAGE

"The rainstorm of last Friday night was one of the most destructive that ever visited this section. The showers of Friday afternoon were followed by heavy rain on the evening, which continued with but slight intermission, increasing in volume, until it seemed as though the heavens were sending down torrents of water. The atmosphere was heavily charged with electricity, and a loud burst of thunder accompanied by vivid lightning plainly indicated that a storm of no small magnitude was raging. The water ran like rivers through the streets of Mineral Point; but up to half past nine o'clock the storm had done but little damage.

The evening passenger train arrived about on time, although the precaution was taken of running somewhat slower, from Calamine up, on account of the rising flood.

The storm which was tremendous everywhere, seemed to have centered northeast of the city, and after what many believe was a water spout, the floods came rushing down the stream upon which Butler's dam is situated...

Flood damage being repaired below Butler Dam. Mineral Point Library Archives

> At about half past nine Butler's dam burst, with a noise like a clap of thunder; and the flood, with irresistible force, swept everything before it. Huge boulders, weighing upwards of a ton, were carried from the walls of the dam, and scattered along the track of the water for a distance of hundreds of feet."

In October 1890, Matt Schmit and his wife, Mary, doubled their investment by selling the mill property to Phil Allen Jr. for $1,300. Allen, along with other Mineral Point businessmen had just organized the Mineral Point Woolen Mill. The men were interested in the old grist mill property for its location and its water resources. They would add a large three-story building to the north side of the grist mill and use the water and its water wheel for the manufacture of flannels and woolen clothing. The up and down history of the Mineral Point City Mill was coming to an end.

The old stone grist mill building was part of the woolen mill operation from 1890 to 1902. When the woolen mill ceased operation in 1902, the buildings sat vacant for over four years. In August of 1906, a new manufacturing plant was started in the buildings, and the old stone grist mill portion of the building was torn down to make way for a railroad spur and siding that was coming up the valley to service the new plant and the upper zinc works.

Mineral Point Library Archives

This circa 1890 photograph was taken from Commerce Street in Mineral Point and looks east up the Darlington Road valley. The Mineral Point City Mill is the split-level stone and frame structure to the right against a bluff and was built in 1845/49. At the time this picture was taken, it was no longer operating as a grist mill but had been incorporated into the large frame building that was added to its north side in 1890. The two buildings combined became the Mineral Point Woolen Mills. The box car near the woolen mill building is on the C. M. & St. Paul Railway tracks just south of the Mineral Point Railroad Depot. Supplies for the woolen mill were carried over the Mineral Point Creek on a small wooden platform bridge.

The building in the middle of the picture shows the ice house built on Butler Dam by Sam Wright in 1880. The spillway for the mill pond can be seen to the buildings left.

The building just above the ice house is the Mineral Point Town Hall which was built in 1860.

CHAPTER 5: MINERAL POINT WOOLEN MILL, 1891–1902

By the last decade of the nineteenth century, the city of Mineral Point was on a roll. Profits from a renewed mining boom created unprecedented commercial and industrial activity in the area. A municipal waterworks had been established, the zinc industry was expanding rapidly, new rail lines were planned and a pulp mill, a new bank and a new high school were about to be built.

Mineral Point was abuzz with excitement in the early months of 1890. There was talk of a woolen mill coming to town that would employ from thirty to forty hands. A stock company was being formed to attain this goal. On April 24, 1890, the *Mineral Point Tribune* reported that a committee comprised of Mayor Joseph LaMalle, John Charles and P. Allen Jr. had gone to Milwaukee to look at a weaving and woolen mill that was for sale. The mill was located in Jackson, a small town northwest of Milwaukee, and the men were going to investigate the possibility of purchasing the mill from a Mr. E. Strickler and moving the equipment to Mineral Point. Mr. Strickler wanted to enlarge the field of his operations with a larger mill, additional capital and a more favorable location. He was willing to sell his equipment and bring it and himself to Mineral Point to help set up a new mill.

After examining the mill and its prospects, the men returned to "Point" and presented their findings to a group of citizens who *"heartily acquiesced"* to secure the mill equipment for a new woolen mill to be built in Mineral Point.

Iowa County Democrat, July 11, 1890

"The Mineral Point Woolen Mill Co. has purchased the plant of Mr. Strickler, at Jackson, and will carry on the business there until suitable buildings are erected at Mineral Point."

A committee which included W. P. Gundry, W. A. Jones and W. J. Penhallegan was appointed to raise the $25,000 required by the state to form a corporation. The money was raised, a corporation formed and articles of incorporation were created and recorded with the office of the Register of Deeds and filed with the Secretary of State at Madison.

Once the articles of incorporation were official, a meeting of the directors of the woolen mills was held on May 23, 1890, and the following officers were elected: *"Philip Allen, Jr., president; Charles Gillmann, vice president; W. P. Gundry, secretary; R. J. Penhallegon, Jr., treasurer; and E. Strickler, superintendent." A second committee was appointed to select a site for the mill, and it is expected that a location will be fixed upon within a few days, when work upon the building will be commenced."*

On August 15, the *Iowa County Democrat* reported that the Mineral Point Woolen Mills had purchased the old Mineral Point City Mill (grist mill) property. The property had been sitting idle since June 20, when a huge flood had burst "Butler's" mill dam and flooded the valley below.

Iowa County Democrat, August 15, 1890

"A SITE FOR THE WOOLEN MILLS"

The board of directors of the Mineral Point Woolen Mills have purchased from Matt Schmit Sr., his mill property, including buildings, "Butler's" dam, and land adjoining. The property is close to the railway track, east of the depot, and will make an excellent site for the new woolen mills. Work will soon be commenced on repairing the dam and erecting the necessary buildings; and the manufacture of woolen cloths will ere long one of the industries carried on at Mineral Point.

Unfortunately, progress on building the new mill was delayed. One of the chief reasons was how to handle the matter of water supply to the mill in the most economical manner. Another slowdown was waiting for R.L. Joiner, the county surveyor, to survey the piece of ground they were interested in.

Once the Mineral Point Woolen Mills announced the purchase of the old grist mill property from Matt Schmit and purchase matters were resolved, the board of directors went right to work with plans for building a woolen mill building.

Mineral Point Tribune, August 28, 1890

NOTICE TO CONTRACTORS

Sealed proposals will be received until 12 o'clock noon, Monday, Sept. 8th, 1890, for the carpenter work in the construction of the Mineral Point Woolen Mills, according to plans and specifications on file at the First National Bank.

The Directors reserve the right to reject any or all bids.

By order of Board of Directors,

Philip Allen, Jr., President.
William P. Gundry, Secretary

Mineral Point Tribune, October 2, 1890

"Work on the new woolen mills is being pushed right along."

Iowa County Democrat, October 3, 1890

"Joseph Ellery & Sons have secured the contract for the carpenter work for the woolen mills."

Iowa County Democrat, October 17, 1890

"A large force of men are at work building the foundation walls of the Mineral Point Woolen Mills. The building will be a three-story frame, 90x48 feet."

Iowa County Democrat, October 24, 1890

PROSPERITY AHEAD

A very favorable tide has set in for Mineral Point. There are evidences on every hand which go to show that from this time on, the city will have a sure and steady growth. It is located in the heart of a very rich agricultural and mining section, and has prospered under the most adverse circumstances. Surrounded, as it is, by new lines of railroad and the numerous villages which have sprung up in the consequence of the building of these new lines, our city still enjoys a large trade and is today a good substantial business center of nearly 3,000 inhabitants.

Mineral Point Library Archives

The Mineral Point City Mill (grist mill), purchased by the Mineral Point Woolen Mills in 1890, is the split-level building to the right against the bluff. At the time this photo was taken, it was no longer operating as a grist mill but had been incorporated into the large woolen mill frame building. The woolen mill was going to use the grist mill water and water wheel for the production of flannels and woolen clothing. The boxcar near the woolen mill building is on the C. M. & St. Paul Railway tracks just south of the railroad depot. Supplies for the woolen mill were carried over the Brewery Creek on a small platform bridge.

Mineral Point Library Archives

The small wooden platform bridge for crossing Brewery Creek can be seen in photo on page 47. It was used to move supplies from railroad boxcars to the woolen mill. The buildings in the distance are part of the Mineral Point Zinc Works.

The following articles are some of the stories that were printed in the local newspapers.

Mineral Point Tribune, December 4, 1890

A carload of machinery a day is being unloaded at the woolen mills this week. The buildings are now nearly completed, and the hum of machinery will soon be the order of the day.

Mineral Point Tribune, February 28, 1891

ALMOST READY

In a week or two, our new Woolen Mills are expected to be in operation. Most of the machinery is in place, ready for connection with the engine. The work of putting in steam pipes throughout the large structure, by which each story is to be heated without the use of stoves or furnaces, was a tedious job, but is now fully completed. By the system of steam heating, danger of fire is reduced to the minimum, and comfort of operatives at all seasons is assured. Minor finishing touches will be put on as opportunity affords after the mill proper is in complete running order. Be not surprised if you hear the whistle of the Woolen Mills engines before another issue of the Tribune.

Iowa County Democrat, March 29, 1891

THE WOOLEN MILLS

The woolen mills are now in operation, although they will not be run to their full capacity for several weeks. The amount of machinery on the several floors of the building convinces one of the fact that the enterprise is by no means small or unimportant. The president, board of directors and Superintendent Strickler are attending to all matters necessary to place the mills in first-class running order. It ought to be a matter of congratulation among our people that the manufacture of flannels and cloths has been added to the industries of Mineral Point.

Iowa County Democrat, June 5, 1891

E. Strickler, the gentleman who superintended the construction of the Mineral Point Woolen Mills, has exchanged his stock in this mill for a small mill in the northern part of the state and has removed to Eau Claire. John Strickler and his two brothers are in charge of our mill, which are now turning out about 400 yards of goods per day.

No reason was given for E. Strickler to exchange his stock and move to Eau Claire. It was not mentioned whether John Strickler and his brothers were related to E. Strickler.

Iowa County Democrat, September 4, 1891

"MINERAL POINT WOOLEN MILLS"

One of the leading institutions of this city, one that is carrying the fame and good fortune of Mineral Point to remote sections, is the big woolen mills of which our city is so justly proud. Mineral Point people can well indulge in feelings of pride over their big mill, as it stands today one of the best equipped mills of its size in the entire country. The buildings of the mill are located on the C. M. & St. P. Ry., near the depot, are four stories high, and covered, both roof and sides, with corrugated sheet iron, making not only a very handsome and substantial building but one from which danger from fire is reduced to the minimum.

The mill proper is a four-story building, 48 x 90 feet in dimension, while the dye house and machine shops find room in a three-story building 24 x 40 feet in dimension. The boiler house is a building 30 x 44 feet in dimension.

Sanborn Fire Insurance Map.
Mineral Point Library Archives

The mill is supplied with all the latest improved machinery, and is running to its full capacity daily. The mill contains two sets of cards, two jacks and ten looms. It is known among woolen mill men as a two-set mill.

The capacity of the mill is 500 yards of flannels daily. It is now turning out that number of yards each day of as good flannels as any other mill in the United States working on the same grade of goods, which product finds ready customers in Marshall Fields and C. V. Farwell, of Chicago. The mill gives employment at present to 26 hands, many of which are girls.

Iowa County Democrat, September 6, 1894

The Mineral Point Woolen Company are putting electric lights in the mills, in order to run at night, it being necessary to do so that orders for goods may be filled on time. The mills were never in better running order, and the product is first class. They are now turning out flannels, stocking yarns, blankets, skirts, cassimeres and sanitary flannels.

Mineral Point Tribune, October 25, 1894

These Mills first ran about January 1, 1891. Like most similar enterprises, its operation developed defects daily, which had to be overcome before any dividends could reasonably be expected. Through '91, '92 and '93 this condition continued. All the capital stock was paid in, and no additional shares could be hypothecated. During this trying time came the election

> of 1892, with democratic success and stagnation of business throughout the country; and pending the inaction of congress, in 1893, the Mineral Point woolen mills shut down... In the summer of 1894 the stockholders resolved to make one more effort to save their investment in the mills, and made plans to resume operations.

The Mineral Point Woolen Mill was a victim of a steep start-up learning curve and negative market forces. Between high tariffs pushing the price of foreign wool higher than was economically feasible to turn a profit, plus competition from "King Cotton," the woolen industry had a difficult time turning a profit.

Iowa County Democrat, April 25, 1895

W. A. Jones, N. H. Snow, W. J. Penhallegan, James Brewer, Calvert Spensly, P. Allen, and R. J. Penhallegan, Sr., have organized as the Mineral Point Manufacturing Company and will operate the Mineral Point Woolen Mills on and after May 1st. The affairs of the company which operated the mill last year will be settled up according to the resolution adopted at the last meeting of the stockholders. The members of the new organization are deserving of praise for the enterprising spirt which they manifest: and as there is a good demand for the product of the mills, it is completely hoped that they will meet with success. The mills are in better shape than ever before for turning out first class fine goods, the operatives are more skilled, and the managers have a great knowledge of the wool manufacturing business. There is therefore a good prospect for the profitable operation of the mills to their full capacity.

Iowa County Democrat, May 23, 1895

The woolen mills started up again on Monday morning, under the management of the Mineral Point Manufacturing Company.

Mineral Point Tribune, February 6, 1896

The Democrat is glad to state upon authority of the stockholders of the new company, that a large number of orders have been received from Chicago and elsewhere, and that the mill will resume operation early in February. The company is showing the finest line of samples ever turned out of these mills; and it is hoped and believed that enough orders will be secured to keep the mills in constant operation during the coming year.

Mineral Point Tribune, March 26, 1896

"Reports say that the Mineral Point Woolen Mills are now running very successfully, orders already received insure active operation through the summer."

The news later in 1896 was not positive for the woolen mills. The McKinley Tariff was injurious to the price of foreign wool for woolen manufacturers who were producing carefully and well-selected fine, sound staple wools. Cotton was taking a larger share of the market, and many woolen mills closed due to falling demand, and orders were not sufficient to start up the machinery. "Shoddy" wool was taking more and more of the woolen goods market. "Shoddy" woolen goods were woolens that had cotton, jute or jute butts, "cows or calves hair" or marsh hay mixed in.

Despite these challenges, the Mineral Point Manufacturing Company was able to keep the looms humming, and in 1896, the woolen mill had an impressive exhibit at the Iowa County Fair.

Iowa County Democrat, September 17, 1896

THE MINERAL POINT WOOLEN M'FG CO.'S EXHIBIT

Among the fair exhibits, the Mineral Point M'fg Co. had a display which reflects great credit upon Mr. Sells as superintendent, for having such a great variety of all new and fancy patterns of his own designing. In ladies' skirt patterns alone there were 120 designs, besides blankets, flannels and Cassimeres, all of which are made from carefully and well selected fine, sound staple wools. No shoddy, cotton, jute or jute butts, cows or calves hair, Bagdad, China wools, or marsh hay are used in their goods. Those wishing to get pure wool goods—just what they buy— will find it greatly to their interests to inquire of their merchants for the Mineral Point goods, which can be had from all the merchants in the city, at one price only. You can get their skirts, either made up ready to wear, or not made up, as desired. They will also scour blankets for anyone wishing such work done.

Some of the last correspondence from the Mineral Point Woolen Manufacturing Company was a letter written on June 24, 1898, by superintendent of the mill, A. G. Sells, to W. A. Nicholas of Livingston, Wisconsin. The first part of this letter goes as follows:

W. A. Nicholas
Livingston, Wisc.

Dear Sir:

Instructive and prices of our goods as follow:;

1st Our fine line of shirts are all made from very carefully selected long staple pure fine domestic wools.

2nd Thus impress upon your trade that when we say wool we mean just what we say. We do not mean part shoddy or nails, or jute or jute butts, or cotton or cotton linters, or Bagdad or China wool, or marsh hay. These are the adulteration that many are using to mix with a small amount of staple wools and then sell them for all wool, etc. ...

3rd Our line has no competition in the way of finish and design as all of the designs are of our own composure, which are very neat and attractive to the eye, and if properly shown, any merchant will see they cannot well pass the line as their beauty will sell themselves ...

The actual letter contains four pages, and it explains in detail the qualities of the woolens manufactured by the company, such as color, sizes and cost. (*Special thanks to Carl Tunestam of Tunestam's Antiques for sharing this letter with me.)*

Iowa County Democrat news brief, July 14, 1898

"The woolen Mills are running night and day to fill the large order for blankets for the U.S. army."

Stores continued to advertise in the local papers for Mineral Point Woolen Company wool skirts, heavy blankets and heavy wool shirting flannels as late as 1901.

Despite making products from *"carefully and well selected fine, sound staple wools,"* the Mineral Point Woolen Manufacturing Company's struggle against negative market forces in the wool industry continued, and on March 22, 1902, the woolen mill was permanently closed. After shutting the mill down, the big woolen mill building sat vacant until late 1906 when inventor George Kelly and local entrepreneur Phill Allen purchased the building and property to establish a plant for the manufacture of vulcanized fiberboard and other rubber goods for use in electrical machinery. The following explanation for the trials and tribulations of the woolen industry appeared in the *Iowa County Democrat*.

Iowa County Democrat, January 26, 1905

As quoted from the Providence Journal

CAUSE AND EFFECT IN WOOL

When the price of woolen goods goes down at the same time that the price of wool goes up we have a pretty conclusive proof that the fleece of the sheep has ceased to be the principal constituent of what is sold as woolen clothing. In the trade papers, indeed, the price of "shoddy" is now as regularly quoted as the price of wool, and it, apparently, is what mainly determines the manufacturer's cost of production.

This entry on the last page of a Mineral Point woolen mill time book was posted by Allen Tucker.

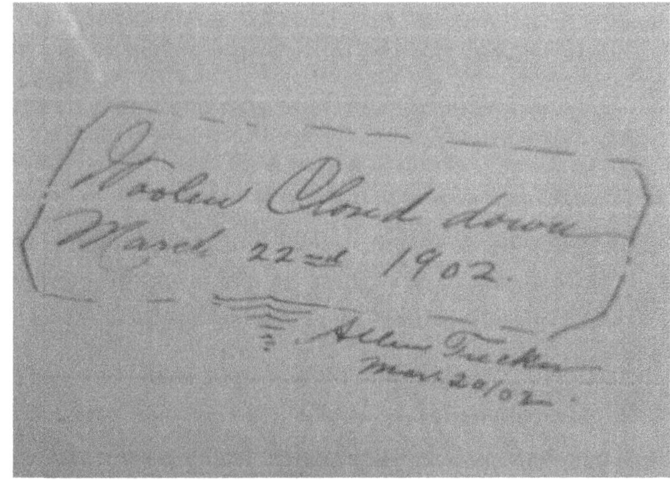

Woolen Closed down
March 22nd 1902.
Allen Tucker
Mar. 20/02.

Courtesy Carl Tunistam's Antiques

CHAPTER 6: BADGER RUBBER WORKS, 1906–1911

After the Mineral Point Woolen Mills closed on March 22, 1902, the buildings fell into disrepair and remained vacant for the next four years. Then in August of 1906, inventor George Kelly and Mineral Point entrepreneur Phil Allen transformed the old woolen mill building into a plant for the manufacture of vulcanized fiberboard and rubber goods. The new enterprise would be known as the Kelly Manufacturing Company DBA Badger Rubber Works. The 1906 Mineral Point tax record lists Kelly & Company as owner of the property.

That same year the Mineral Point Zinc Company was building a switchback railroad spur up the Darlington Road valley in order to reach the company's upper oxide plant a short distance to the south. To do this the old stone grist mill was torn down, and tracks were laid between the rubber plant and the bluff. The tracks would then cross a double-trestle bridge over Mineral Point Creek above Butler's Dam [*Iowa County Democrat*, 10/26/1905] and continue up the valley where they reversed course, crossed over a second bridge and climbed up and around the bluff to reach the upper oxide plant which was being enlarged and improved.

Mineral Point Library Archives

This circa 1908 photo shows the newly refurbished old woolen mill building with window glass replaced and a fresh coat of paint. A 100-foot chimney was built to vent a large new boiler, and additions on the east end of the building provided needed space for the new Badger Rubber Works. Fresh cuts in the earth past the rubber plant and around the bluff show the new roadbed that was built for the zinc works railroad spur.

Iowa County Democrat, August 9, 1906

AN EXTENSIVE MANUFACTURING PLANT

TO BE ESTABLISHED IN MINERAL POINT, ON THE SITE OF THE OLD WOOLEN MILLS, NEAR THE DEPOT

VULCANIZED FIBER BOARD

AND OTHER RUBBER GOODS FOR USES IN ELECTRICAL MACHINERY TO BE THE PRODUCT

WORK ON BUILDINGS BEGUN

A new enterprise has been started in Mineral Point. Work is going on at the old woolen mills building which surely means something. A representative of the Democrat learned that it means the establishment of a plant for the manufacture of vulcanized fiber board and other insulating electrical goods. The main part of the present building will be utilized, but the south part of the old plant (the old grist mill) is being torn down. To the east of the machinery building there will be erected an engine room 20 x 30 feet, and the boiler room 30 x 40 feet, with a driveway between these buildings. The new buildings, smoke stack and coal sheds are to be of brick. Some of the machinery for the plant has already arrived, including two boilers, each of 150 horse power. Three car loads of brick have arrived for building purposes; and also a car load of cement which is to be used in making concrete foundations for the machinery, which is to be placed in position as soon as the buildings are made ready to receive them. The machinery is to be run by a very large Corliss engine. It is proposed to make the plant a permanent one for Mineral Point. It will be equipped with the best of machinery, including rubber mixer rolls which weigh over 30,000 pounds. George Kelly (the well-known inventor and patentee of asbestos car linings, and insulating materials) and Phil Allen are the leading spirits in the enterprise. Their insulating goods have been subjected to the most rigid electrical trials, and have stood tests of 30,000 volts without breaking down; and this at such places as the Lewis institute in Chicago. The manufacture of asbestos car linings and material for cold storage plants carried on here a few years ago by Messrs. Kelly and Allen was transferred by them to Winona, Minn., and to a city in Indiana. The plants at these places have steadily grown and now have a daily capacity of 75,000 feet of car lining and 25,000 feet of material for cold storage buildings. Orders for these materials are received from all parts of the United States.

Vulcanized fiberboard was invented by British inventor Thomas Taylor in 1859. It was a tough, resilient, hornlike material that was produced from 100 percent cellulose material such as cotton, linen rags or wood pulp. Up to eight paper plies saturated with zinc chloride were used to build up the desired fiber thickness, and it was then pressed together under high pressure to promote bonding. Then and now, the board can be produced up to 3/8 inches thick and can be sheeted or wound up into rolls. Vulcanized fiber board has a high insulating value and is used as electrical insulating material, gaskets for sealing pipe unions and washers, and packing materials. There is no rubber in vulcanized fiberboard.

Unlike fiberboard, rubber is manufactured from latex, which in the early 1900s was harvested from the Hevea tree (rubber tree) in South America by indigenous rainforest dwellers. The liquid latex was smoked and heated by the natives to form chunks that could be sold at ports and shipped around the world. Large chunks of this raw rubber were delivered to the Badger Rubber Works on railroad cars. The factory then cured the raw rubber in a process called vulcanization, invented by Charles Goodyear in 1839. The finished rubber had a higher tensile strength, a resistance to swelling and abrasion and was more elastic. The rubber then became suitable for processing hoses, tires, industrial bands, sheets, shoe soles and other products.

Iowa County Democrat, October 18, 1906

The work of transforming the old woolen mills building into a plant for the manufacture of vulcanized board, and other goods for electrical uses, is being carried steadily forward under the direction of George Kelly. The brick building for the boiler room is almost completed, as is the building for the large engine, which is shortly to be installed therein. Two boilers, (each of 150-horse power), and one smaller boiler, have been placed in position. Bricklayers are at work on the smoke stack, which is to be one hundred feet in height.

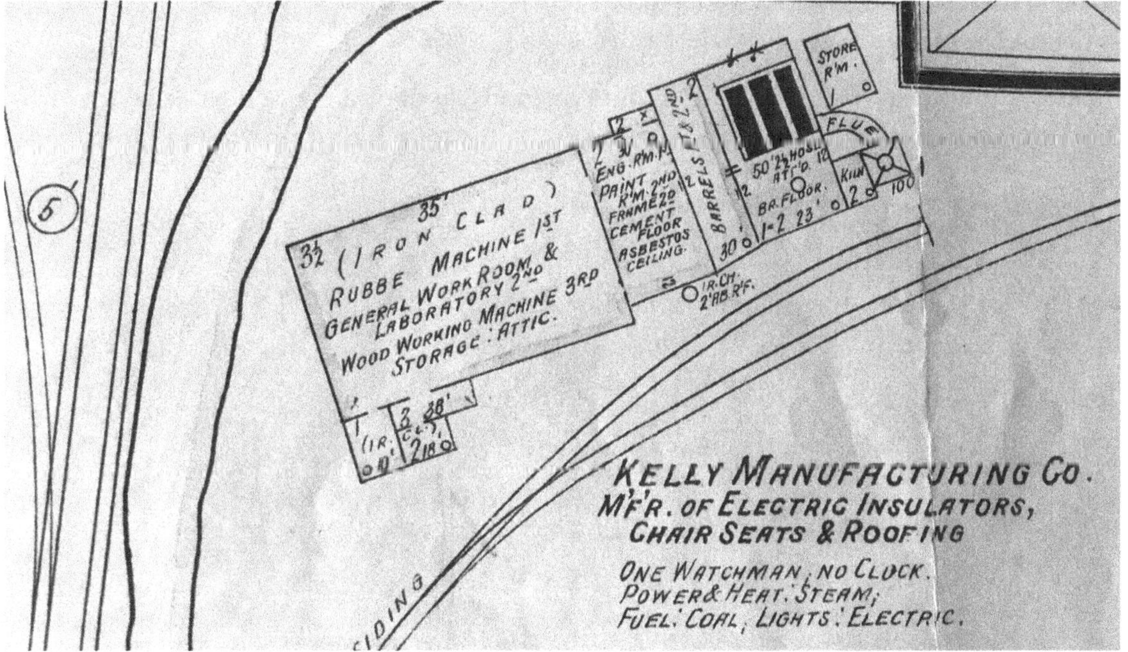

Wisconsin Historical Society, Madison, Wisc.

This 1908 Sanborn map shows the layout of the Kelly Manufacturing Company. The building was iron clad and had coal-fired boilers to supply steam heat. Electricity had recently been run to the building from the zinc works power plant for lighting. Machinery, raw materials and other supplies as well as coal for the boilers could be delivered from railroad cars on the new siding, and finished products could be loaded onto the cars and shipped out of Mineral Point.

Iowa County Democrat, November 8, 1906

The old woolen mills have been resurrected from the junk heap, painted, glass restored to all the window frames, new brick additions have been made, a brick smokestack going up 100 feet high and all to put onto a solid basis the new vulcanized fiber board plant promoted by the inventor, George Kelly, and the dean of the Republican Party in Iowa County, Phil Allen, prince of good fellows.

There has been no beating of tom-toms, nor house-top cries of another big industry launched in the zinc city, but thousands of dollars are going into the new plant just the same and it is rapidly nearing completion.

Iowa County Democrat, April 11, 1907

The Kelly Manufacturing Company has commenced operations, but are not as yet going in full blast.

Mineral Point Tribune, December 5, 1907

Mr. and Mrs. Joseph Bahl came here (Mineral Point) from Dodgeville last week to make their home in this city. They have moved into one of the new Horn Jenkins houses. Joe has a job at the rubber plant.

This circa 1907 photo shows the Mineral Point Railroad Depot and the Badger Rubber Works deep in a December snow when Joe Bahl was moving to Point for a job at the rubber plant.

Mineral Point Library Archives

This circa 1908 photo is taken from the hillside southeast of the rubber plant and is looking west toward town. The old woolen mill building has been painted, and the new brick engine room, boiler room, and 100-foot brick chimney have been completed. The railroad flat cars with riders are on the zinc spur that climbs the hill and rounds the bluff above the rubber plant to reach the reconstructed and enlarged oxide plant just south of the rubber plant.

Mineral Point Library Archives

Mineral Point Tribune, August 5, 1909

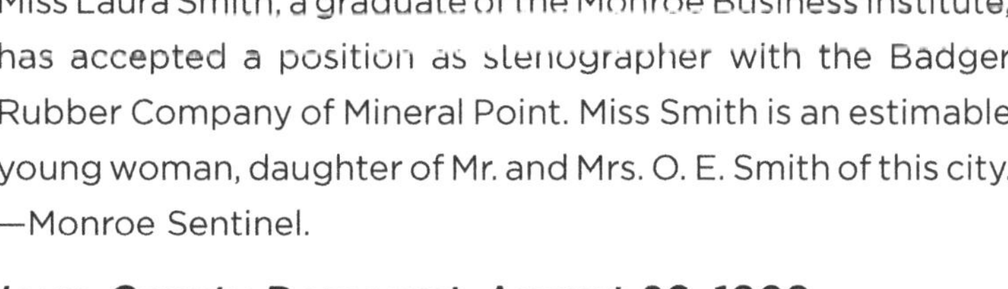

Miss Laura Smith, a graduate of the Monroe Business Institute, has accepted a position as stenographer with the Badger Rubber Company of Mineral Point. Miss Smith is an estimable young woman, daughter of Mr. and Mrs. O. E. Smith of this city. —Monroe Sentinel.

Iowa County Democrat, August 26, 1909

A GREAT INDUSTRIAL SHOW

HELD IN MINERAL POINT FROM AUGUST 17 TO AUGUST 20, INCLUSIVE

A SUCCESS, FINANCIALLY AND OTHERWISE

EVIDENCES OF PROGRESS ON EVERY HAND

EXHIBITS OF WISCONSIN'S BLUE GRASS REGION A REVELATION TO VISITORS

FIRST AND BEST FAIR

Industrial hall presented a beautiful appearance, with its many fine displays. Dealers in and out of Mineral Point city were well represented in the building, and vied with each other making neat displays of their goods and wares. The progress which Mineral Point is making was especially shown by the display of electrical power and electrical utensils of various uses, and by the display of rubber goods manufactured in Mineral Point by the Badger Rubber Company. These displays were truly a revelation to many of Mineral Point's advancement towards an industrial center.

By the end of 1909, the Badger Rubber Works was bucking economic and financial headwinds.

Raw rubber which could be purchased on the open market for as little as 35 cents a pound a year ago was now selling for as much as $2.10 a pound and becoming appallingly scarce, with no prospect of a price decline in sight. [*Iowa County Democrat*, 11/18/1909]. This huge increase in the price of raw rubber surely impacted the company's profits.

In addition to these price increases, Mineral Point was thrown into economic turmoil in late 1909. On October 11, the First National Bank of Mineral Point was suddenly closed. Phil Allen, who was president of Badger Rubber Works and head cashier at the bank, had been embezzling funds from the bank for many years. He had looted the accounts of hundreds of the bank's depositors, including businesses such as the Badger Rubber Works. Allen was charged with forgery, falsification of books and reports, abstraction, larceny and embezzlement. Allen, dean of the Republican Party and loyal backer of Mineral Point businesses, was convicted of his crimes and sentenced to 10 years in the United States Penitentiary at Leavenworth, Kansas.

Unfortunately, the owners of the Badger Rubber Works could not free themselves from these developments, and the company was sold at auction the next year. The following story appeared in the March 31,1910 *Mineral Point Tribune*.

Mineral Point Tribune, March 31, 1910

TAKE OVER RUBBER FACTORY

The Badger Rubber plant of this city, including buildings and machinery, sold to the highest bidder in consequence of the Phil Allen bankruptcy proceedings, has passed into the hands of Messrs. L. A. Ross, R. G. White and G. A. Graham, they having offered the highest price therefore.

Iowa County Democrat, March 24, 1910

RUBBER INDUSTRY

BADGER PLANT PURCHASED BY L. A. ROSS, R. G. WHITE, AND G. A. GRAHAM

NEW MACHINERY ADDED

WORKS WILL BE IN FULL OPERATION WITHIN A FEW DAYS

March 24, 1910—The Badger rubber plant has been purchased by L. A. Ross, R. G. White and G. A. Graham. It will now be known as the Ross Rubber Manufacturing Company and will manufacture hose, belting, packing, tubing, gaskets, fruit jar rings, mats, mattings, plumbers' supplies, diaphragms, moulded goods, pump valves and automobile tires.

Mineral Point Library Archives

On last Saturday the Badger Rubber plant, including buildings and machinery, passed into the hands of L. A. Ross, R. G. White, and G. A. Graham, they having offered the highest price therefore.

The new proprietors are men of push and business enterprise, and are determined to make the plant a winner. The company will be known as the Ross Rubber Manufacturing Company.

In addition to the extensive machinery already in the works, a car load of new machinery is on track, and will be put in place as soon as possible, to enable the company to fill orders received for rubber goods. The company's manufacture includes hose, belting, packing, tubing, gaskets, fruit jar rings, mats, matting, plumbers' supplies, diaphragms, mounded goods, and pump valves.

In addition to the articles named the company will manufacture automobile tires as soon as the necessary machinery can be placed in the works.

Mr. Graham, who is in charge of the plant, is an expert in the manufacture of rubber goods.

This fact is shown by the large number of orders which have been placed with the company for rubber supplies of various kinds.

The plant, when in full operation, will give employment to many hands, and it is to be hoped the proprietors will meet with the success which their enterprise merits.

Mineral Point Tribune, April 14, 1910

RUBBER PLANT UNDER FULL HEADWAY

The Badger Rubber Works of this city, after a forced idleness in consequence of the tangled condition into which it was thrown by Bank-Buster Allen's manoeuvring, (sic) is again a busy institution. The new proprietors have a large working force employed and the prospect for a rapid increase in business is very encouraging. These works should, and it is believed will, prove a boon to Mineral Point.

Iowa County Democrat, May 12, 1910

INVENTION IN RUBBER MANUFACTURING

George N. Graham, manager of the Ross Manufacturing Co., is applying for a patent at Washington for a process of reclaiming waste rubber. The material after treatment can be used with or without the addition of new rubber in the manufacture of mechanical rubber goods. He is also applying for a patent for the treatment of the fabric or lining of auto tires, wherein by using this process the rubber is thoroughly impregnated into the fabric so that the various plies will not separate, thus lessoning (sic) the risk of blowouts. Another advantage is that tires made by this process can be made cheaper than the old method.

Iowa County Tribune, January 26, 1910

Mr. Geo. N. Graham, general manager of the Ross Rubber Manufacturing Company of this city, has resigned his position with the company and accepted a position as general manager with the Federal Rubber Company of Cudahy, Wis. He will enter his new position at once. Mrs. Graham will join her husband in Milwaukee about March 1.

Mineral Point Tribune, March 2, 1911

FIRE! FIRE! FIRE!

THE ROSS RUBBER PLANT COMPLETELY WIPED OUT

At about 2 o'clock Wednesday morning of this week fire broke out at the Ross Rubber Plant located near the depot in this city, and in two hours was completely wiped out. The untimely hour and location made it impossible for fire fighters to successfully combat with the flames.

The origin is unknown. Will Brenton, the young man employed as engineer and who chanced to be at the plant because of the regular night watch being sick, cannot account for the fire in any way. It was discovered in a nook of the building near a window which is seldom if ever open, but at this time was found open.

The plant was valued at about $30,000. Insurance but little, hence the loss is heavy. L. A. Ross and R. G. White, both of this city, were the owners. To the dozen or more employees who are out of employment in consequence, the fire will prove a considerable inconvenience.

Mineral Point Library Archives

The 1912 date on this photo is incorrect. The fire occurred March 1, 1911, and was reported in the March 2 paper. The building was only insured for $18,000. The plant was valued at $30,000 and was considered a total loss. $30,000 in 1911 dollars would equal over $822,000 in 2020 dollars. This was a devastating loss.

Mineral Point businessmen stood in disbelief on the zinc works railroad spur surveying the fire damage. The only part of the rubber plant standing intact after the fire was the 100-foot brick chimney, which still stands today as a sentinel of Mineral Point's past commercial history.

Iowa County Democrat, March 2, 1911

FACTORY BURNED

THE ROSS RUBBER WORKS TOTALLY DESTROYED EARLY WEDNESDAY MORNING

TOWN HALL IGNITED

BUT FIREMEN PUT OUT THE FIRE AND SAVED ALL BELOW THE ROOF

The great plant of the Ross rubber works of Mineral Point was totally destroyed by fire early Wednesday morning. The alarm was sounded shortly before 2 o'clock, and the firemen promptly responded and soon had strong streams of water playing on the burning building. But the fire had gained such a headway and the structures and contents were so flammable that it was impossible to save the plant. Fortunately the wind blew from southwest to northeast and swept the flames and burning cinders away from the adjoining lumber yards, railway station and town. With the water at hand, cars and other property close by were saved.

The town hall of the town of Mineral Point, nearly a quarter of a mile distance caught fire; but the firemen went out (with) ladders, and with water from the creek nearby, (Mineral Point Creek), saved all but the roof of the building.

The rubber plant, which was almost totally destroyed, was insured for $18,000.

Mineral Point Library Archives

This account of the rubber plant fire was written by Mineral Point author and resident, Lester Dunnwiddie. His book, "From Home—When the Whistles Blew," is archived in the Mineral Point Public Library Archives.

Businesses of the Past

THE OLD RUBBER PLANT

Let us think back to the City of Mineral Point some years ago to conjure in our mind a picture of the old rubber plant. It was a brick building located about one fourth mile south of the old depot. It was built back against the hill on the east side of the valley where the railroad track was located. It was a large building; and one notable feature was the high smoke stack, which was used to supply the right draft for the large steam boiler that supplied power and heat for the plant.

There was a side track on the railroad that switched off the main line enabling the loading of both processed and raw rubber on the cars for transportation out of Mineral Point.

I remember the excitement the night the plant caught on fire from some mysterious origin. It was along about midnight.

A locomotive was fired up and took off for Darlington to bring back some firefighting equipment to help put out the fire.

Some days after the fire some of the boys salvaged sheets of rubber and cut them into shoe sizes. They nailed them to their shoe soles making them up to one and a half to two inches thick.

One old landmark of this rubber plant was the ruins of the tall smokestack as it stood many years—a relic of the past.

There were always many questions as to what started the fire. The general opinion of arson was involved. There had been cases of suspected arson down through the history of Mineral Point. Some were proven, others still a mystery. If I remember right, this investigation into the rubber plant fire continued for several years, and nothing was ever proven resulting in no convictions.

The old rubber plant chimney still stands today, 114 years after it was built. It is a relic of Mineral Point's past commercial history. The goose on top of the chimney is watching over its nest on Gratz's Pond below.

John Sharp 2018

CHAPTER 7: ZINC OXIDE PLANT RAILROAD SPUR, 1906–1930

Mineral Point began its raucous boom and bust history as a mining town in 1827 when large quantities of galena were found on Mineral Point Hill. As the miners dug these deposits of lead ore, they also found a lightweight yellow rock which they called "dry bone," since it resembled partially decayed bones. This byproduct of the lead mines was burdensome and thought to be worthless by the miners, so they tossed it onto the overburden piles, not realizing it had value as a mineral.

Then in 1857, two German scientists touring the region recognized the discarded light-yellow rock as zinc carbonate, which contained 52 percent metallic zinc. As the years passed and the mining of lead began to decline, the production of zinc carbonate increased. By the middle 1870s, the mining of zinc carbonate soon outpaced the production of lead, and it wasn't long before Mineral Point had a zinc oxide plant to process zinc carbonate.

In 1883, William Jones and his two brothers bought the Mineral Point Zinc Company which had been organized in 1882 and grew it into the largest zinc oxide works in the United States. Southwest Wisconsin and Mineral Point were fast becoming a booming zinc mining region and smelter town. Large quantities of zinc carbonate from Southwest Wisconsin and other zinc mining regions around the country were being shipped to the Mineral Point Zinc Company to be processed and converted into white zinc oxide, the basic ingredient of good paint. In order to handle the large amount of zinc carbonate that was coming into the Mineral Point Zinc Company for processing, expanding the zinc oxide plant became a necessity.

The expansion of the oxide plant to process more ore was a huge undertaking for the Mineral Point Zinc Company. Besides reconstructing, enlarging and improving the plant, the company wanted to deliver ore and coal by rail to the hillside above the plant, where it could be dumped into the new bins that were being built below. This made the unloading of the ore and coal more efficient and saved time. Achieving this would involve building a railroad spur, excavating a large cut in the limestone hillside above the plant and constructing a 1,000-foot long by 15-foot high stone retaining wall.

Figuring out how to get to the upper oxide plant was no small task for the engineers designing this spur. Tracks above the oxide plant would be 35 feet above the main railroad line on the valley floor, and locomotives would be required to pull heavily loaded ore and coal cars up a maximum 2.2-percent grade to get there.

It was determined that leaving the main line north of the zinc works and going east one-half mile up the Darlington Road valley past the rubber plant was the best route to take. To do this, the old stone grist mill would need to be torn down, and the tracks would pass between the bluff and the rubber works, cross over Mineral Point Creek on a trestle bridge and continue up the valley, ending near the old stone culvert on Darlington Road. The trains would then reverse course, switch onto a second track, cross over a second trestle bridge next to the first bridge and wind their way around the bluff above the rubber plant and continue on to the upper oxide plant at a more or less level grade.

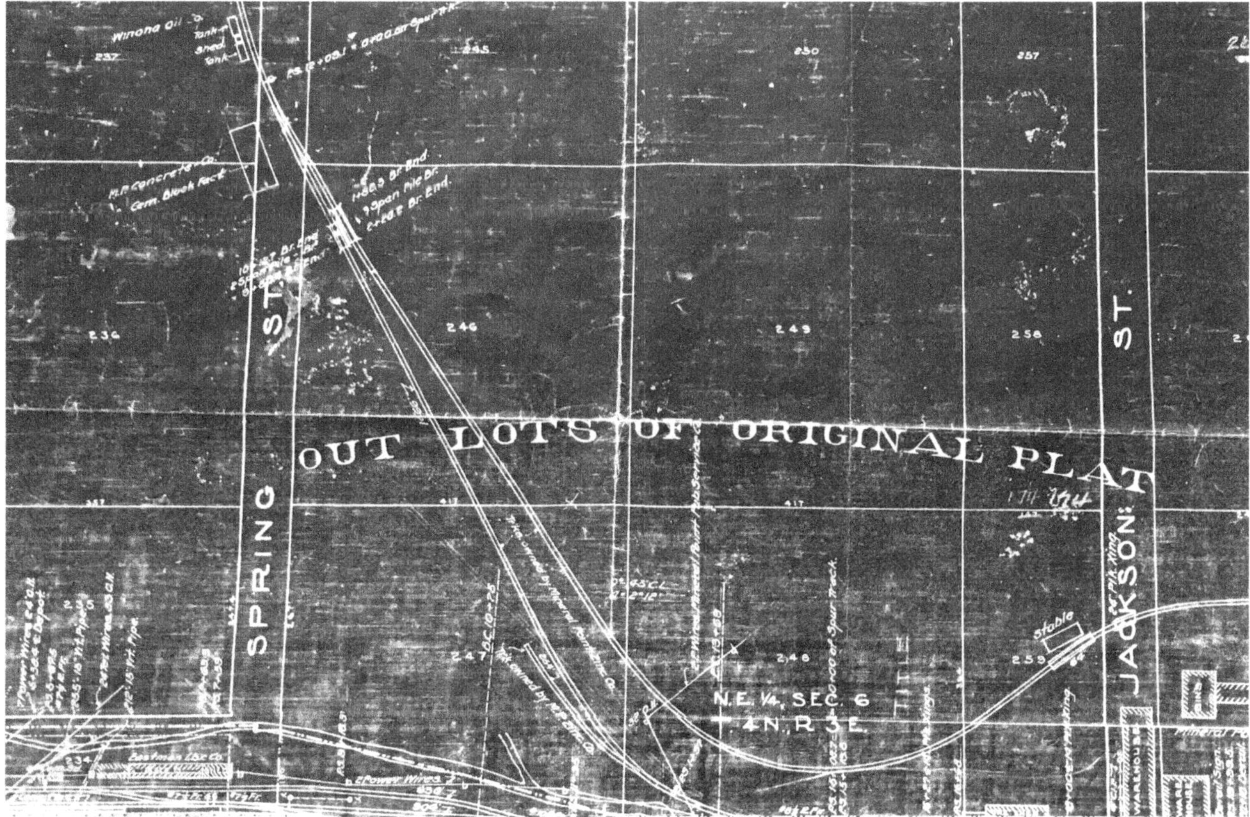

Mineral Point Library Archives

This 1916 Chicago, Milwaukee and St. Paul Railroad station map shows the route of the zinc company spur as it leaves the main line and heads east one-half mile up the Darlington Road valley to near the city line. The map also shows the siding that was constructed for the rubber plant and the two trestle bridges over Mineral Point Creek. The steepest part of the spur was where it wound its way up and around the bluff above the rubber plant.

The map also shows the location of the Mineral Point Concrete Construction Company (1909/1921), and the fuel tanks owned by the Winona Oil Company (circa 1916), both of which were served by the rail spur. The grade and tracks for the spur were built by the Mineral Point and Northern Railway Company, which at that time was owned by the Mineral Point Zinc Company.

This Mineral Point and Northern steam engine is moving flat cars on the hill above the rubber plant. This was the steepest section of track on the zinc company spur.

Remains of the old trestle bridge pilings from the Mineral Point Zinc Company railroad spur that crossed over Mineral Point Creek can be seen in this 2018 photo. The spur was built in 1905 to deliver zinc ore to the upper oxide plant.

John Sharp 2018

Iowa County Democrat, March 17, 1904

A BRIGHT OUTLOOK

THE YEAR 1904 TO MARK A NEW ERA IN MINERAL POINT'S INDUSTRIAL PROGRESS

ADDITION TO ACID PLANT

OUR CITY IS THE CENTER OF A REGION ABOUNDING IN AGRICULTURE AND MINERAL WEALTH

The spring season of 1904 opens with signs of progress for Mineral Point and surrounding country. Men of means have been examining mine prospects hereabouts, and some investments have lately been made, which indicates an activity in mining in the near future. The introduction of modern machinery will greatly aid in the development of this section, which is known to be rich in lead and zinc ores. The extensions and improvements which are

> being made to Mineral Point's great oxide and acid plant prove that the city will continue to be the leading market for the ores from the Wisconsin zinc fields and for ores from distant points as well.

Zinc carbonate was shipped to Mineral Point for processing from as far away as New Mexico and Colorado.

> ### *Iowa County Democrat,* April 20, 1905
>
> **THE OXIDE PLANT**
>
> **TO BE RECONSTRUCTED AND GREATLY ENLARGED AND IMPROVED**
>
> **EXTENSIVE BUILDING OPERATIONS**
>
> **ADDITIONAL GROUND PURCHASED FOR NEW FURNACES, STOREHOUSES, AND OTHER BUILDINGS**
>
> **THE EAST SIDE**
>
> "The work of reconstructing and enlarging The Mineral Point Zinc Company's great oxide plant in the city is under way. It will entail, perhaps, the most extensive building operations ever accomplished in Mineral Point in a single year. The scene of activities will be on the east side of the railway. A spur track will be run along the side of the bluff east of the works and up the track all the coal and ore for the oxide plant will be hauled.
>
> Several acres of land south of the bag rooms and the cooper shops have been purchased from George Jeuck, Fred Gollner, R. N. James and others: and upon this land will be erected blocks of furnaces, store houses, and other buildings."

The new oxide plant and portions of the 1,000-foot-long retaining wall are shown in this circa 1908 photo. The retaining wall was built to hold back the hillside east of the plant. The rail spur ran

Mineral Point Library Archives

along the top of the wall and above the oxide plant and was engineered so trains could deliver coal and ore to this upper level and then dump it over the wall into bins below. Portions of the rock wall and railroad bed remain today. Mineral Point can be seen to the north through the haze created by the zinc works.

Mineral Point Library Archives

Iowa County Democrat, May 4, 1905

A great force of men and many teams are at work on the improvements at the Mineral Point Zinc Works. The great steam shovel employed to tear out the sides of the everlasting hills is an object of great interest to our citizens. There is greatly increased industrial activity at the oxide plant as the Democrat said in advance there would be.

Iowa County Democrat, October 26, 1905

A GREAT WORK

A PORTION OF THE HILL ON THE EAST SIDE OF THE OXIDE PLANT REMOVED TO MAKE WAY FOR RAILROAD TRACKS

ONE THOUSAND FEET OF WALL

ALL MATERIAL FOR THE PLANT TO BE UNLOADED FROM THE NEW TRACKS

THE WORK TO CONTINUE

Mineral Pointers do not have to go away from home to see how railroads are built in the mountains. Within the city limits there is a fine example of such engineering.

"The work of excavating for tracks of the Mineral Point and Northern, to run on the east side of the oxide plant, was begun early last spring and has been carried forward ever since.

> A steam shovel was kept at work for several weeks along the sand bluff approaching the plant from the south; and the material taken out was hauled in train loads along the track of the Mineral Point and Northern from Highland Junction west, for ballasting the roadbed. For the last three months the work of excavating, building walls, and grading for the new tracks has been under the supervision of J. R. Land, of Monroe, and during this time thirty men and from twelve to fifteen teams have been constantly employed. Just east of the oxide plant was the hill of limestone, and this has been quarried back about twenty feet. Over one thousand feet of stone wall has been built, an average height of which is about fourteen feet. The tracks will be at an elevation of thirty-five feet from the land on which the kilns and new buildings of the oxide plant are to be erected. In order to reach the upper grade two tracks are to be built to the bridge across the stream (Mineral Point Creek) above Butler's dam, from which point trains will be run to the plant. The work that has been done indicates the extensive additions and improvements that are to (be) made to the oxide plant. It means much not only to Mineral Point but to the entire lead and zinc region of Wisconsin."

The above article was not exaggerating when it said, *"Mineral Pointers do not have to go away from home to see how railroads are built in the mountains."* Excavating the roadbed for the zinc spur was a daunting task for the engineers. Locomotives would be required to pull their heavily loaded ore and coal cars up a grade that rose 35 feet from the valley floor to the upper oxide plant. Besides removing huge amounts of limestone when excavating the roadbed above the oxide plant, the giant steam shovel had to remove tons of dirt and rock when cutting the roadbed around the bluff above the rubber plant. The forward progress of cutting away the hillside with a steam shovel mounted on a flat car, then laying track to move ahead, and then digging more hillside, was a slow process that took weeks. The Mineral Point and Northern began grading and digging the roadbed for the new spur in 1905, but crews did not start laying ties and track above the oxide plant until 1908.

Mineral Point Library Archives

This circa 1908 photo shows a steam crane mounted on the railroad flat car above the oxide plant. The crane was used to place huge limestone boulders that had been quarried along the hillside to build a 1,000-foot-long limestone wall. The crane also unloaded and placed large equipment into the plant below. Portions of this wall and roadbed remain today.

Iowa County Democrat, May 7, 1908

MINERAL POINT IS ALL RIGHT

THE GREAT ZINC WORKS TO BE MADE STILL GREATER

TRACK ON THE EAST SIDE

WORK OF LAYING TIES AND RAILS IS UNDERWAY

TWO LARGE INDUSTRIES

> "Work is now being carried on at the zinc works which means much for the future of Mineral Point. On Monday morning a force of men began laying ties and rails on the east side of the oxide works, where extensive grading was done two years ago. Completion of this track will enable the company to haul ore, coal and other supplies up the great hill east of and overlooking the works, where delivery to the furnaces below can be made mainly by gravitation."

Large portions of the 1,000-foot-long great wall and smelter tailings remain today just south of Ivey Construction Company.

John Sharp 2020

The enlarged and upgraded Mineral Point Zinc Works continued to prosper along with Mineral Point for the next several years. In 1927, the market price for zinc carbonate was high, and the oxide plant was running at full capacity. Several trains a week traversed the zinc spur to reach the upper oxide plant. The mining of zinc carbonate in the region had grown to an all-time high. Then in 1928, dark clouds were on the horizon, and life was about to change. The amount of zinc carbonate being mined declined, and the price for zinc oxide had fallen sharply. In October of 1929, the stock market crashed. A year later in September 1930, the Mineral Point Zinc Company closed the oxide plant. The glory days of the mining industry and *"mountain railroads"* in Mineral Point had come to an end. The upper oxide plant railroad spur that had taken so much planning and work to construct was abandoned and neglected. The huge cut in the hillside above the zinc works remains to this day.

The tracks of the lower zinc spur going up the Darlington Road valley stayed in use until 1946, servicing the Mineral Point Concrete Construction Company, the Mineral Point Oil Company, the Winona Oil Company and the Dave Fine salvage yard. Dave loaded scrap iron into railroad cars from 1940 to 1946. In 1946, Dave bid on and won salvage rights to remove the bridges over Mineral Point Creek and the spur tracks east of the bridges. Once the tracks were removed, Dave leveled the railroad bed on the east side of the creek to make more salvage yard area. [This information was gathered on a phone conversation with Paul Fine in February of 2009. Paul lives in Milwaukee, Wisconsin, and is one of Dave Fine's sons who worked at the salvage yard.]

Details in this 1925 aerial photograph show Darlington Road rounding the bluff just east of the Mineral Point Railroad Depot. A locomotive and railroad cars can be seen crossing Mineral Point Creek on a Mineral Point and Northern trestle bridge, and the old "Depot Quarry" that was mined in the 1850s for limestone blocks to build the Mineral Point Railroad Depot is shown on the south hillside. The businesses shown along Darlington Road are the Mineral Point Oil Company, which later became the Chad Harker Stock Yard and a Standard Oil gas station run by Joe Filardo and Joe Garcia of Mineral Point. Both businesses are circa 1930.

Wisconsin Historical Society Reference Library

CHAPTER 8: WHITNEY SMITH TANNERY, 1860-1876

In 1844 and at the age of 40, Whitney Smith immigrated with his family via Stark County, Illinois, to Mineral Point, Wisconsin. Like most immigrants at that time, Whitney was looking for more opportunity and a better life for his family in a changing world. Mineral Point was a booming mining town in 1844 and certainly offered opportunity to men like Whitney Smith and his family. "Point," as the town was known back then, just incorporated as a village, and Wisconsin would soon be admitted to the union in 1848 as the 30th state.

Whitney was born July 14, 1804, and was raised in the frontier town of Wilkes-Barre, Wyoming Valley, Pennsylvania. As a young man, he served an apprenticeship at the tanning trade and then engaged as a tanner and merchant. After leaving Wilkes-Barre, he would again become a tanner and a merchant in Mineral Point.

Whitney Smith arrived in Mineral Point as a man of means and soon became active in the community. He built a home for his family on Fountain Street, started a mercantile business, dealing in general merchandise that included everything from dry goods and groceries to "Farrell's Celebrated Arabian Liniment, a sovereign remedy for man and horse." By 1848, he had become secretary of the Mineral Point Masonic Lodge and president of the Mineral Point Merchants' Association.

Mineral Point Library Archives

Whitney built this house for his family on Fountain Street circa 1849/1850. The house still stands at 224 Fountain Street in Mineral Point. The two-story center section of the home is log construction, and Smith may have added the side wings on to this older cabin. The present owner has exposed the log construction.

The part of town where Whitney built his house was very well known in the early days of Mineral Point due to a spring that ran pure and cold with potable drinking water. The spring is located a short distance up Fountain Street from the Smith household and became known as Jerusalem Springs. Early settlers built shacks and cabins near the spring, one of which may have been the cabin Whitney added on to. It was a luxury in those early days to have a home so near water, and the water bubbling from the spring ran down the valley right in front of the Smith household. A close look at the home photo faintly shows the stream entering under a small wooden bridge in the front yard as it passes underground for a short distance.

Water was required to tan hides, and it can be speculated that Smith located his home near this stream with the idea that he would eventually be tanning hides again. Unfortunately, the spring and stream have since been buried in a storm pipe and now runs underground.

During the same time Whitney was building his house on Fountain Street, he started his mercantile business. This ad for his new business located on High Street was placed in the December 1847 *Wisconsin Tribune*. This same ad was placed in the *Tribune* from 1847 until 1854.

***Wisconsin Tribune*, December 10, 1847**

WHITNEY SMITH,

DEALER IN MERCHANDISE IN GENERAL

Agent for the sale of Flour, Provisions,

PATENT MEDICINES, &c. &c.

Mineral Point W. T.

Years after the mercantile business was established, Whitney opened an auction and commission room on High Street. The ad for this business reads as follows:

***Mineral Point Tribune*, February 26, 1856**

WHITNEY SMITH,

AUCTION & COMMISSION MERCHANT, WILL ATTEND PROMPTLY TO SALES OF GOODS, MERCHANDIZE

(Merchandise) &c., &c., at his Old Stand, on High Street, Mineral Point, Wisconsin.

He will also receive Goods, Merchandize, and Produce on Storage, or sell on Commission.

Although it is not certain when Whitney began tanning hides in Mineral Point, one of his earliest ads gives the location of his tannery at "Carter's Stone Block, Fountain St., Mineral Point." "Carter's Stone Block" was a carriage and wagon business run by John Carter in a two-story stone building at 222 Fountain Street. This carriage and wagon shop was right next door and to the east of the Smith home on Fountain Street. Although there is no history of a tannery on Fountain Street prior to Whitney Smith's 1859 ad, surely with his experience as a tanner he was doing a small amount of tanning at John Carter's wagon shop before this.

Whitney prepared this ad for what he called his "New Tannery" in 1859. The advertisement stated that *Whitney Smith is now prepared to purchase hides and peltries, or to tan them on shares at* "Carters Stone Block," *Fountain St., Mineral Point.*

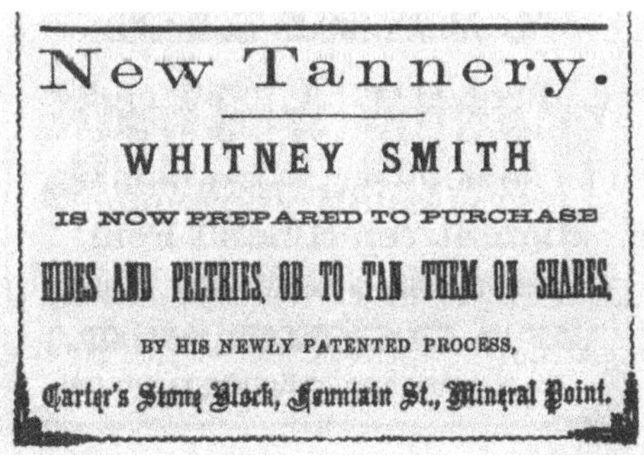

Directory of the CITY OF MINERAL POINT for the year 1859, compiled by T.S. Allen.

The following year he placed a "Mineral Point Tannery" ad in the October 1860 *Mineral Point Weekly Tribune*. This ad locates the tannery on Fountain Street "below Henry Alley," which is very close to Carter's wagon shop and his home.

Mineral Point Weekly Tribune, October 9, 1860

Eventually Whitney outgrew his neighborhood leather tanning operation, and it became necessary for him to look for a new location, preferably out of town, where he could build a tannery to process more hides and meet the growing demands for his leather goods. Due to the methods used in tanning hides in those days, a large tannery would not have been welcomed in town. The tannery business was an unglamorous and smelly profession, and it was usually located on the outskirts of town near water. Water was required in the tanning business. Animal skins were first softened in water and then scraped to remove excess fat and hair. After the skins were softened and the fat and hair removed, they were soaked in vats of urine and animal dung or brains. Once this soaking was completed, the skins were beat and kneaded to make them soft and supple. Finally, they were tanned with a chemical compound called tannin, derived from tree bark and certain plant leaves. This process was known as vegetable tanning. Whitney had experience as a tanner in Pennsylvania, and he knew that it would be best to build a larger tannery outside the city limits.

On July 5, 1860, Whitney leased a plot of land for his new tannery from Matilda Hood. The plot was located just east of the depot on outlot 246 (Harrison's Survey, City of Mineral Point). This parcel was on the "outskirts" of town, and the tannery would be located on the south bank of Mineral Point Creek, near water. His new tannery business would not be a smelly bother to townspeople in this location.

The following abstract gives details of Whitney Smith's land lease from Matilda Hood. Oliver M. Sanford is shown as a co-lessee, and he may have been taken on as a partner when the new tannery was built. His name would again appear three months later in an advertisement for their retail "Leather Manufactory" located on the northeast corner of High and Commerce streets, Mineral Point.

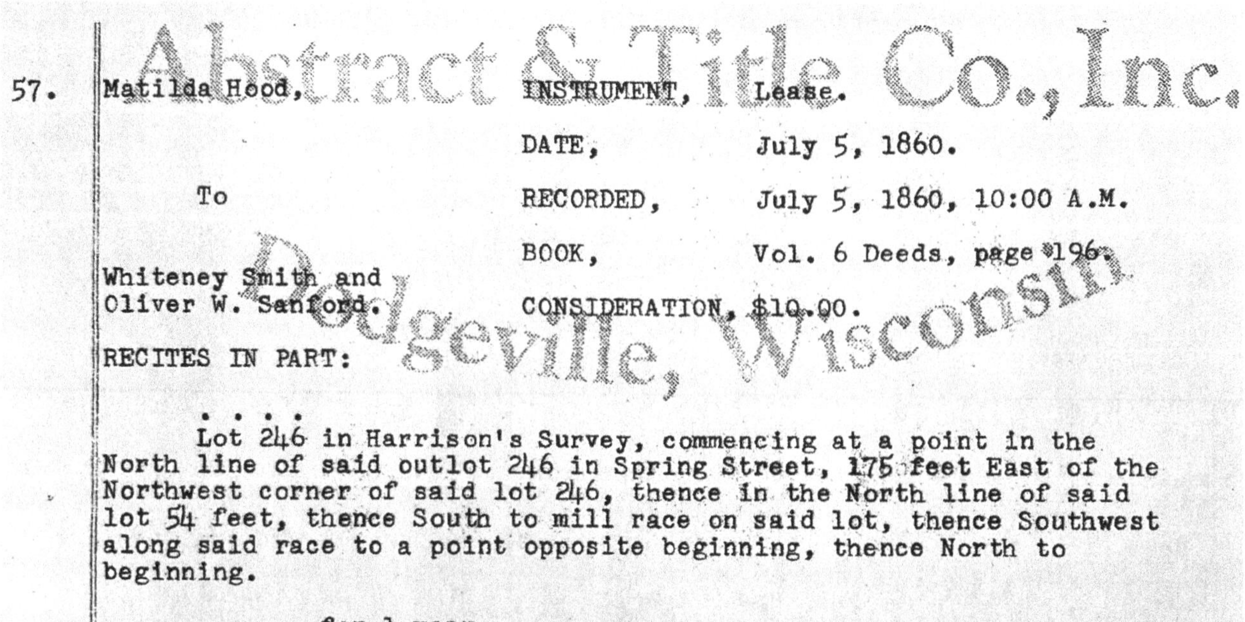

Abstract & Title Co., Inc.
Dodgeville, Wisconsin

57. Matilda Hood, — INSTRUMENT, Lease.
DATE, July 5, 1860.
To — RECORDED, July 5, 1860, 10:00 A.M.
BOOK, Vol. 6 Deeds, page 196.
Whiteney Smith and Oliver W. Sanford. — CONSIDERATION, $10.00.

RECITES IN PART:

. . . .
Lot 246 in Harrison's Survey, commencing at a point in the North line of said outlot 246 in Spring Street, 175 feet East of the Northwest corner of said lot 246, thence in the North line of said lot 54 feet, thence South to mill race on said lot, thence Southwest along said race to a point opposite beginning, thence North to beginning.

. . . . for 1 year.

Soon after the lease was signed, construction of the new tannery began.

Mineral Point Weekly Tribune, July 31, 1860

New Tannery—Mr. Whitney Smith, has erected a new building for a Tannery near the Mill Pond, a short distance from the Depot, and has it nearly ready for business. The leather manufactured by Mr. Smith is giving general satisfaction, and to keep up with the wants of the trade he has found it necessary to enlarge his business to a much greater extent than he at first anticipated.

The following portion of the 1871 Taylor & Willets Map of Mineral Point shows the location of Smith's Tannery along Darlington Road on the south bank of Mineral Point Creek.

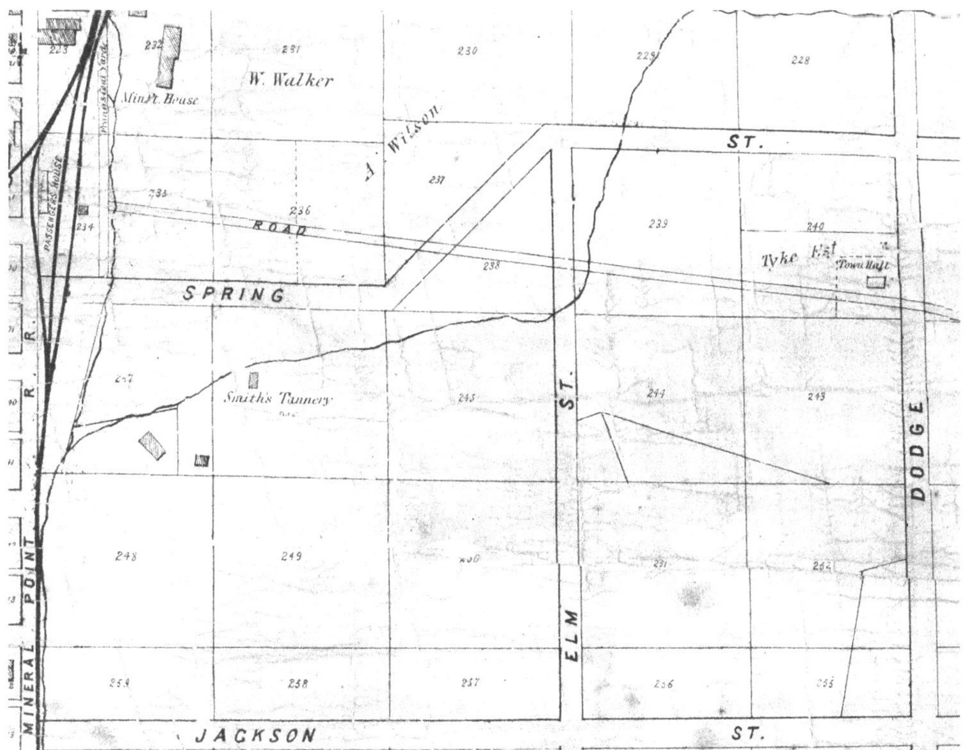

Mineral Point Library Archives

After getting his new tannery working, Whitney Smith and Oliver Sanford opened a new retail leather store in Mineral Point.

The following 1861 ad (page 78) in the *Mineral Point Weekly Tribune* shows Oliver M. Sanford as a partner in the "Leather Manufactory" and gives the address of the new retail livery leather store as the northeast corner of High and Commerce Streets, Mineral Point. The ad also states that plastering hair is always on hand. Plastering hair was scraped from horse and cow hides during the tanning process and was then employed for making plastering mortar to give it a fibrous quality and help it hold together.

***Mineral Point Weekly Tribune*, July 12, 1861**

LEATHER
MANUFACTORY.
:o:
Whitney Smith,............Oliver W. Sanford.

THE SUBSCRIBERS TAN AND FINISH
HARNESS, BRIDLE, BELT,
COLLAR & STRING LEATHER;
Also, KIP, CALF and SHEEP SKINS

Which they will sell at the lowest rates for CASH, at their shop, North east corner of High and Commerce streets, Mineral Point.

☞ They will pay the highest price for GOOD Beef Hides, Horse Hides, Kip, Calf and Sheep Skins.

For JOB TERMS see our Card.

SMITH & SANFORD.

N. B. Plastering Hair always on hand. 1o-tf
Mineral Point, March 1st 1861.

The "Leather Manufactory" was a small, dark brown frame building with a sign hanging between the upstairs windows above the front door which read "W Smith." Animal skins and pelts appear to be hanging by the front entrance. Whitney could sell his tanned leather goods at this in-town store.

Mineral Point Library Archives

Whitney entered his leather products in the 1867 Iowa County Fair and received these favorable comments in the *Mineral Point Weekly Tribune.*

Mineral Point Weekly Tribune, October 9, 1867

COUNTY FAIR.

We are pleased to chronicle the fact that the Iowa County Fair was a perfect success and met the expectations of its friends... The leather manufactured and presented by Whitney Smith of this City, received much praise and deserved commendation from all who examined it. It was but the ordinary finish of all Leather sold by Mr. Smith, without any extra touch to make it attractive, and yet it was pronounced by all judges to be a superior article that would have done credit to any of the large manufacturers of the East.

The last mention of Whitney Smith and his tannery appeared in a news article on September 9, 1869.

Mineral Point Tribune, September 9, 1869

Tannery,—We happened into Whitney Smith's tannery on Saturday, and found our old friend very busy, but complaining that there is a lack of the encouragement necessary to make his business what it should be. We are very sorry for this, as it always sounds harshly to us to hear of failure to patronize any home enterprise. Mr. Smith is confident that if manufacturers would give his leather a fair trial they would find it equal to any eastern (leather). We hope they will do so.

Whitney Smith, at the age of 72, took leave of his tannery business in 1876 and moved to Chicago, Illinois, where he lived with his wife, Anna, for the next three years, visiting with old friends and living the big-city life.

Whitney's partner, Oliver W. Sanford, joined the Union army in 1861 and that same year lost his life in the Civil War battle at Antietam, Sharpsburg, Maryland. Oliver had a brother named Francis Sanford who also lived in Mineral Point, and he undoubtedly worked at Whitney's tannery alongside Whitney and brother, Oliver. Interestingly enough, Whitney's wife, Anna, and Francis's wife, Caroline, were sisters.

Francis and Caroline left Mineral Point in 1867 and moved to Richland County, Wisconsin, where Francis purchased and ran a tannery for a few years. The following year, they sold their Mineral Point home and a lot on High and Commerce Streets.

"Good fortune" followed Anna and Caroline, for in 1877, they received an unexpected large inheritance from a brother in Mexico. The following Mineral Point Tribune article tells of this good fortune.

Mineral Point Tribune, April 04, 1877

GOOD FORTUNE, WELL DESERVED

By the demise of a brother in Mexico, Mrs. Whitney Smith, of this city, and Mrs. Frank Sanford, formerly a resident here, but for some years residing in Richland Center, and two other sisters, become possessors of quite a large fortune. Rumor places each sister's share at $10,000 to $25,000. The many friends in the vicinity of Mrs. Smith and Mrs. Sanford, and their highly esteemed husbands, will rejoice at this intelligence. No people more deserving were ever favored by dame fortune.

A $25,000 inheritance in 1877 would be equal to $663,000 dollars to each sister in today's money, and it certainly afforded the Smiths and Sanfords an opportunity to consider making life changes, which they did.

Three months after the inheritance, Whitney announced that William Martin was succeeding him in his tannery business, and in July, while still living in Chicago, Whitney and Anna put their Mineral Point home up for sale.

Mineral Point Tribune, June 13, 1877

"Try what you will, there's nothing like leather." Having full confidence in this motto of our craft, I am determined to show it by engaging in the manufacture of leather, as the successor of Whitney Smith, at his old stand, where I am willing and ready to buy hides, or tan them for others on equitable terms. Call or write for further particulars. Try me, and then judge for yourselves.

Wm. Martin

Mineral Point Tribune, July 18, 1877

For sale—my house and lot on Fountain Street, in Mineral Point, at low figures, and easy terms.

Whitney Smith

By 1877, Francis Sanford was no longer running his Richland Center tannery business, and soon after Caroline had received her inheritance, he established a livery business and ran a stage line between Richland Center, Viola and other area towns.

Whitney and Anna left Chicago in 1879 and moved to Richland Center to be near the Sanfords, where Anna and Caroline could be together and live a family life.

In 1879, Whitney's livery and leather business at the foot of High Street also changed hands.

Iowa County Democrat, August 1, 1879

Kirkpatrick & Shears carry on the livery business at Whitney Smith's old stand foot of High Street.

Whitney and Anna lived in Richland Center for six years, and in 1885, Whitney's health began to fail, and after a long and honorable life, he passed away at the age of 82.

Iowa County Democrat, November 27, 1885

The Richland Republican of last week contained the following in regard to a former resident of this city: Whitney Smith, one of the oldest and most respected citizens of this village is very low. He is gradually sinking under the weight of old age.

Iowa County Democrat, December 4, 1885

WHITNEY SMITH

In Richland Center. Nov. 19, 1885, Whitney Smith, in the 82d year of his age. Mr. Smith was born in Wilkes-Barre, Wyoming valley, Pa., July 14, 1804. He came west in 1835 and settled in Stark County, IL, naming the town which grew around him after his old home, Wyoming Valley. Leaving Illinois in 1844, he came to Wisconsin, and located at Mineral Point, in which place he remained until 1876. In 1879, after three years residence in Chicago, Mr. Smith came to this place, where he has since resided. During forty-five years of his life he was actively identified with interests of the church.—Richland Republican.

Whitney Smith lived a long and honorable life and was a well-respected citizen of Mineral Point. He contributed in many ways to making Mineral Point the vital and key town that it was during the middle 1800s in southwest Wisconsin.

CHAPTER 9: MINERAL POINT TOWN HALL, 1860–1913

On August 17, 1848, three months after Wisconsin gained statehood, the state legislature met and passed an act which divided Wisconsin into 72 counties, one of which was Iowa County.

This act also required the Board of County Commissioners in each county to meet on the second Tuesday of January, 1849, and divide their respective counties into convenient townships. Thus, boundaries for the Town of Mineral Point were formed, and the clerk of Iowa County notified inhabitants of said town to meet on the third day of April, 1849, to choose town officials. Parley Eaton, Thomas Riddle and Cyrus Woodman were elected supervisors. Parley Eaton was elected to the office of Chairman of the Board.

Once town officials had been elected, notice of a *Special Town Meeting* to be held at the Mineral Point Courthouse on the 8th day of May, 1849, was posted in three of the *most public places.* This was to be the first town meeting for the Town of Mineral Point.

The following is a true copy of the notice posted in three of the most public places, including the *Wisconsin Tribune,* notifying inhabitants of the meeting.

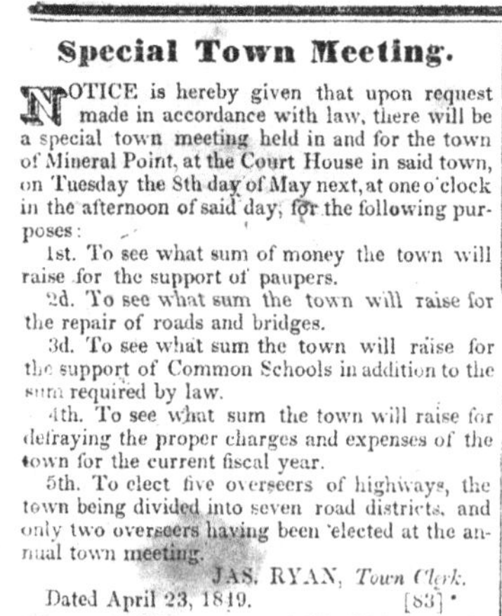

Special Town Meeting.

NOTICE is hereby given that upon request made in accordance with law, there will be a special town meeting held in and for the town of Mineral Point, at the Court House in said town, on Tuesday the 8th day of May next, at one o'clock in the afternoon of said day, for the following purposes:

1st. To see what sum of money the town will raise for the support of paupers.

2d. To see what sum the town will raise for the repair of roads and bridges.

3d. To see what sum the town will raise for the support of Common Schools in addition to the sum required by law.

4th. To see what sum the town will raise for defraying the proper charges and expenses of the town for the current fiscal year.

5th. To elect five overseers of highways, the town being divided into seven road districts, and only two overseers having been elected at the annual town meeting.

JAS. RYAN, *Town Clerk.*

Dated April 23, 1849. [83]

In pursuance of said notice, a town meeting was held at the Courthouse in the Village of Mineral Point on Tuesday the eighth day of May, 1849.

Since the Town of Mineral Point did not have a town hall as of yet, the supervisors continued to hold town meetings at the courthouse in the Village of Mineral Point. When the Village of Mineral Point became a city on March 2, 1857, the town supervisors needed to find a new meeting location, and in 1857 and 1858, town meetings were held at Mathew Goldworthy's home. The 1859 and 1860 town meetings were held at the Graysville School.

The old Graysville School as a home in 2019. John Sharp

At the April 3, 1860 town hall meeting, a motion was made by Henry Skillenger to build a new town hall, *not to exceed four hundred dollars in cost.*

8 On Motion of Henry Skillenger That a town Hall be built and not to Expend four hundred dollars in Cost Motion Carried

9 On Motion of William Noble the Town board to Constitute the Building Committee for Town Hall

10 On Motion of Amos Hays resolved that said Hall be built as near the center of said town as practicable and have it on a road

11 On Motion it was left to the discretion of Town board

April 3, 1860 Mineral Point Town Hall minutes.

A new town hall was built, *not to exceed four hundred dollars in cost... near the center of said town... on a road* (Graysville Road, later named Darlington Road). The first Mineral Point town meeting was held in the new town hall on April 2, 1861.

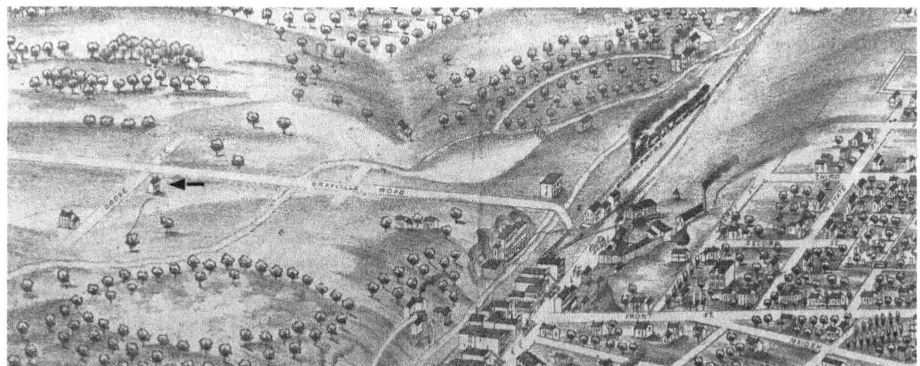

The arrow on this 1872 Bird's Eye View map points to the Mineral Point Town Hall. Mineral Point Library Archives

The Mineral Point Town Hall, middle center, was built in 1860 for $400. It was located one-half mile east of the Mineral Point Railroad Depot on Graysville Road *(Darlington Road)* near what is now the intersection of Old Darlington Road and Highway 39/23.

The Town of Mineral Point met at the new Darlington Road Town Hall from April 2, 1861, until March 8, 1913, a period of 58 years.

The arrow on this 1908 Wisconsin Geological and Natural History Survey map marks the location of the Mineral Point Town Hall located where Darlington Road forked to go north on Dodge Street (Merry Christmas Lane) or south to Darlington.

As the years passed, It became more and more inconvenient to hold meetings at this location, and town residents desired a better place to gather.

Mineral Point Town Minutes, March 1, 1913

A petition was filed by the necessary number of qualified voters of the Town of Mineral Point petitioning for an election concerning the Vacating and removal of the place of election and town meetings, from the present Town Hall to the City of Mineral Point.

Mineral Point Town Minutes, March 8, 1913

Notice of special election is hereby given to the electors of Mineral Point Town, in the County of Iowa, State of Wisconsin, that a special order and election will be held in said town, at the same time and place of the annual election and town meeting on April first, 1913, to submit the question by ballot to the voters of said election, of vacating and removal of the place of election and town meetings, from the present Town Hall to the City of Mineral Point. And for the provision of building, purchasing, or otherwise, of a suitable place or building to hold town meetings and elections in. Also to submit to the electors of said Town of Mineral Point—the question of raising money, not to exceed the sum of two thousand dollars ($2000.00) for the purchasing, building or otherwise of a place to be used for a Town Hall in the City of Mineral Point—levying a tax for the year 1913 or the issuing of bonds for the same.

Dated this Eighth day of March, 1913

Iowa County Democrat, March 20, 1913

A RIGHT GOOD VOTE

TO LOCATE THE MINERAL POINT TOWN HALL IN THE CITY

A LITTLE EARLY HISTORY

COMBINED WITH GOOD REASONS WHY TOWN ELECTIONS AND TOWN MEETINGS CAN BE CONVENIENTLY HELD IN THE CITY

The Town of Mineral Point was organized under state government in the year 1849 comprising the town and the city.

The city charter obtained in 1856 making it a separate municipality, the remaining portion still being the town, under the old name retaining the old records of early days of which the present city was the center; the annual reports of finance, the minutes of board meeting, and the record of roads, radiating from the common center along our principal outlaying streets are among these, and to some people fond of early history, makes very interesting reading.

After the separation of the city, the town held board meetings and elections at various places among which Mathew Goldworthy's residence and Graysville are mentioned for until the present town hall was built in the year 1860 east of the city on the Darlington Road.

A resolution was passed to have it as near to the center of town as possible and still be on a public road. At the time it served its purpose to the people, who held the arrival of caucus day, town meetings and election day as events not to be thought lightly of in those pioneer times. At the time of building the town hall, the hillside surrounding it and for miles beyond was covered with trees and brush, giving shelter to teams and people that gathered there in the stormy weather experienced often about the time of spring and fall election days.

At the present time every tree and bush is gone and the old hall stands on a hillside exposed to bleak winds from every direction, and in its very dilapidated condition, unfit to remain in, as sometime is necessary for many hours at a time transacting business of the town, and holding elections as required by law.

Without going into the matter of what the law was at the time the old hall was built, the present law says, "Town Meetings and elections may be held in any city or village entirely within or adjoining the town."

The logic of the situation at the present time is that the average farmer has more cares, more business and is nearer abreast of the rush and swing of the world than those of years ago.

To the busy man, time is money and convenience is everything and to say the least, the location of the town hall is most inconvenient.

On election and town meeting days of the Town of Mineral Point at least every one attending also makes a trip to this city on business bent or otherwise, and all excepting those traveling the road past the hall have to drive to the city first, where their teams are tied in sheltered places, or in other ways well taken care of. Many entering the city from the Darlington Road do not stop on passing either way to vote on account of their teams, having to get out in the mud, no place but wire fences to tie to, and heated horses from long drive on the incoming trip.

After reaching the city many do not care to walk back through the mud and those coming in on other roads are the same, to record their vote, personally they think only one out of so many, but after all only a small number of such sometimes decide the policy of a state, nation or the destiny (of the) world.

At caucuses and more especially at spring elections, while the poles are temporarily closed to give place to local town affairs, and transaction of necessary business, the room being full, many are compelled to stand outside no matter how much they are interested in the proceedings.

At such times the sentiments of those outside is unanimous for a larger room.

A move has been made to take advantage of the right of the town to hold all town meetings in city and the question will be put up to the citizens of the town at the coming election to procure suitable quarters conveniently located within the city to hold all elections and town meetings in.

This is a move in the right direction and we hope it will succeed.

In addition to the woes mentioned above, at 2 o'clock in the morning on March 1, 1911, burning cinders from the Ross Rubber Plant fire one quarter of a mile away were carried by a strong southwest wind, landing on the roof of the town hall and setting it ablaze. Firemen from the rubber plant blaze rushed to the town hall, and with ladders, buckets and water from Mineral Point Creek nearby, saved all but the roof of the building.

Iowa County Democrat, March 27, 1913

SPECIAL ORDER AND ELECTION

Notice is hereby given to the electors of the town of Mineral Point, in the county of Iowa, state of Wisconsin, that a special order and election by ballot, will be held at the time of the annual town meeting and election on April 1st, 1913, submitting the question to the voters at said election, of vacating, and removal of the place of election and town meetings from the present town hall to the city of Mineral Point, and for the provision of building, purchasing, or otherwise, of a suitable place or building to hold town meetings and elections in.

Also to submit to the electors of said town of Mineral Point the question of raising money not to exceed the sum of two thousand dollars for the purchasing, building, or otherwise, of a place to be used as a Town Hall in the city of Mineral Point by levying a tax for the year 1913, or the issue of bonds for the same.

A petition for such order and election having duly been made to me by more than twelve qualified voters of said town, in writing, specifying the object of such special order or election.

Given under my hand this eighth day of March, 1913 John R. Wallis, Town Clerk.

On April 1,1913, a vote was taken to vacate and remove from the Darlington Road Town Hall and to locate at a new and suitable town hall in the City of Mineral Point.
99 votes were in favor of removal and 41 against.

Iowa County Democrat, April 3, 1913

TOWN DECIDES ON QUESTION

OF CHANGING THE PLACE OF MEETING TO MORE CONVENIENT PLACE

WILL ACQUIRE SUITABLE ONE

Election was an important one as Two important Questions were decided upon—Voted a $500.00 Levy for Improvement of Roads by a vote of 37 to 1... The proposition to establish a town hall within the city carried. This is a good move, and will prove a great convenience to the citizens of the town, who have long conducted the important business of local self-government at great disadvantage in the old town hall on the hillside east of town.

Iowa County Democrat, July 3, 1913

PURCHASE A TOWN HALL

On the West Side of Commerce Street.

The town board of supervisors, James Watters, M. F. Schaaf and Mont. Kendall have purchased from Mrs. Grace Ivey a building on Commerce street, to be used as a town hall for the town of Mineral Point. Locating the hall at a convenient point in town will prove a great public convenience.

On April 7, 1914, the Town of Mineral Point met at its new town hall located at 206 Commerce Street in the city of Mineral Point. At this town meeting, a motion for disposal of the old town hall was left with the town supervisors. There is no record of what they decided.

Iowa County Democrat, October 16, 1913

TOWN HALL BEING FITTED UP

**NEW LOCATION WILL BE ON WEST SIDE OF COMMERCE STREET—
WILL BE VERY CONVENIENT**

The new town hall for the town of Mineral Point, which is in the city, on the west side of Commerce Street, is being painted and fitted up for the convenient transaction of public business.

John Sharp 2019

The building in the previous picture is a portion of the new 1914 Mineral Point Town Hall that was located at 206 Commerce Street, Mineral Point, Wisconsin.

The two-story section of this building is believed to be the original 1860 Mineral Point Town Hall. It is also believed that after it was abandoned it was moved to this site on the Charles Pierson farm sometime between 1914 and 1948. It is located at 4059 STH 39, and today is occupied as a residence.

John Sharp 2019

CHAPTER 10: LIME KILN (MINERAL POINT CREEK), CIRCA 1850/1900

This interesting looking structure is a lime kiln, and its design is more specifically known as a "draw Kiln." These kilns were used to burn limestone rock (calcium carbonate) to produce a form of lime called quicklime. Quicklime was then processed into hydrated lime and it had multiple uses. This kiln's exact location is not known, however, old photos and an 1862 historical document indicate that it was situated a short distance east of town on Mineral Point Creek just below Butler dam.

Mineral Point Library Archives

"Draw kilns" were usually stone structures similar to the kiln shown here. They were loaded from the top with alternate layers of medium sized lump limestone and a fuel such as wood or coal. This combination of limestone and fuel was called a "charge." Lump limestone was used inside of the kiln so the charge could "breathe" during firing and not collapse under its own weight, extinguishing the fire. Once loaded, the kiln was ignited at the bottom, and the fire gradually spread upwards through the "charge." During the firing a chemical reaction called calcination turned the limestone into quicklime. When the charge was burnt through, the quicklime at the bottom of the kiln was cooled and then raked out through a draw hole. Further layers of stone and fuel could be added to the top of the kiln to extend the firing if desired. These kilns usually took a day to load, three days to fire, two days to cool and a day to unload. A temperature of around 900 degrees centigrade or higher must be reached to create the chemical reaction that produces quicklime.

Once quicklime was processed into hydrated lime, it acted as a binder when mixed with sand and water to make mortar. Hair scraped from cow and horse hides could also be added to the mortar to give it a fibrous quality which helped hold it together. The lime made in this kiln was surely used to make mortar that was used in the construction of stone buildings in Mineral Point.

Beside being mortars key ingredient, lime was and is used in agriculture to "sweeten" the soil by raising PH, and in the days of dirt roads lime was spread on muddy ground to firm up the surface. Lime is also a sanitizer. During the 1850 cholera epidemic in Mineral Point people took steps to clean the streets, alleys and cellars and then spread lime as a disinfectant.

Recorded historical evidence of this kiln located on Mineral Point Creek can be found in "The Report on the Geological Survey of the State of Wisconsin," Volume I, January 1862, by James Hall and J. D. Whitney. This report makes mention of a lime kiln "half a mile up the Mineral Point branch." The calcareous beds of buff limestone found along the south side of the valley were favored for burning to make quicklime. This information along with photographs found at the Mineral Point Library Archives give solid clues as to the location of this kiln.

Mineral Point Library Archives

This view of the kiln looking east shows the ramp used for loading the top of the kiln with lump limestone and fuel. To the left of the long wooden building is a structure that appears to be a portion of the Butler Dam spillway, and above the spillway structure on the hillside can be seen piles of earth that remained after quarrying the Depot Quarry in the 1850's. These features would indicate the kiln is located on outlot 246 just below the dam.

The (Circa 1890) picture on page 92 looking west under the lime kiln ramp towards town shows a building that appears to be the Mineral Point City Mill (grist mill) before the large wooden woolen mill building was added.

These three pictures and the mention of the lime kiln in the Geological Survey publication support the probable location of this kiln along Mineral Point Creek just east of town.

Unfortunately, information such as who built and operated this kiln, when it was built and the years it was in operation have not been found. A possible businessman in the near area who may have built this kiln was William Walker who also built the Walker house in 1860. According to the 1881 History of Iowa County, Walker also "engaged in manufacturing lime, and carried on that business for some years."

Mineral Point Library Archives

CHAPTER 11: SAM WHITE WAREHOUSE, 1868–1915

When the first train rolled into the Mineral Point Railroad Depot in 1857, it was the beginning of an exciting and prosperous new era for the town and surrounding area. The Mineral Point Railroad connected with the Illinois Central Railroad in Warren, Illinois, whose rails connected with Chicago and all points east and south. This created access to unlimited markets, and Mineral Point became a major shipping and receiving center. Freight began arriving and leaving the Mineral Point railroad yards daily. In 1858, the railroad shipped 4,591,933 pounds of wheat. By 1860, Wisconsin's rich farm land was producing the second highest wheat yield in the U. S., and wagonloads of grain were coming into town faster than they could be shipped out. More warehouse space was needed to hold incoming and outgoing freight. The following *Mineral Point Weekly Tribune* articles tell of the increased economic activity in Mineral Point and the shortage of warehouses and storage space.

Mineral Point Weekly Tribune, October 14, 1863

Business in Mineral Point is becoming unusually active. Our warehouses are filled with grain, and still it continues to pour in upon us. The streets are constantly filled with loads of wheat, corn, oats and potatoes, &c., all of which bring high prices in cash, to the great joy of the farmers. The Mineral Point Railroad runs an extra train daily, to carry off the produce, but cannot get cars sufficient to keep up with the amount brought for shipment.

Mineral Point Weekly Tribune, October 30, 1867

A large amount of Grain is finding a market here, at liberal prices. The only trouble with buyers is to get cars to ship off the grain as fast as they desire. Every warehouse in the city is literally full, and still the grain comes in. New buildings are going up for the purpose of storing; and Grain, Cattle, Hogs, &c., are being sent off as fast as cars can be had. Saturday last was one of the busiest days of the season, but each day of the week the streets are filled with teams and the stores with customers.

Mineral Point had two large warehouses in 1863 that fronted on Commerce Street and extended back to the railroad track for easy loading and unloading of railroad boxcars. They were the Cobb Warehouse at 23 Commerce Street, built in 1854, and the Lanyon & Sons Warehouse at 121 Commerce Street, built in 1859. This was not enough storage space to handle the large amount of incoming and outgoing railroad freight. The railroad could not move freight fast enough, and the need for more warehouse space was apparent. Five new warehouses would be built over the next few years, including the Sam White Warehouse.

Sam White was a Cornishman who was born in the county of Cornwall, England, November 11, 1815. He immigrated to America and Mineral Point in 1846, spending the entirety of his life here with the exception of a few years spent in California and the Lake Superior mining regions. The 1850 and 1860 census listed him as a miner. Upon returning to Mineral Point, he saw the need for more storage space, and he purchased land from Cyrus Woodman and his wife, Charlotte, on March 22, 1864, with the idea of building his warehouse.

The following abstract gives a legal description of the land Sam White bought from the Woodmans to build his warehouse.

Cyrus Woodman and Charlotte F. Woodman, his wife,	INSTRUMENT,	Warranty Deed.
	DATE,	March 22, 1864.
To	RECORDED,	April 26, 1864, 3:30 P.M.
	BOOK,	Vol. 9 Deeds, page 561.
Samuel White.	CONSIDERATION,	$500.00.

CONVEYS:

Part of outlot 235, Harrison's Survey, Mineral Point, beginning at the Southwest corner of said outlot, thence East along the South boundary of said lot to a point 30 feet distant from the Southeast corner thereof, thence North 43 feet, in a straight line to a point in the West boundary line of said lot 135 feet from the place of beginning, thence along said line to the beginning. Subject to any right of easement which public may have for a highway. Second party is to have no right to use Spring Street unless road thru lot 235 is abolished.

The land was located on Graysville Road, (now Old Darlington Road), approximately 200 feet east-southeast of the Mineral Point Railroad Depot. After crossing the railroad tracks and Brewery Creek, the warehouse was the first rock building on the south side of the road. The footprint was approximately 50′ x 40′. The west end of the warehouse had access to railroad cars by a platform which crossed over Brewery Creek. The large two-story building had a slightly pitched gable roof, and the walls were constructed of random coursed ashlar limestone and sandstone. The following portion of the 1872 Bird's Eye View of Mineral Point shows the Sam White Warehouse on what was labeled Grayville Road.

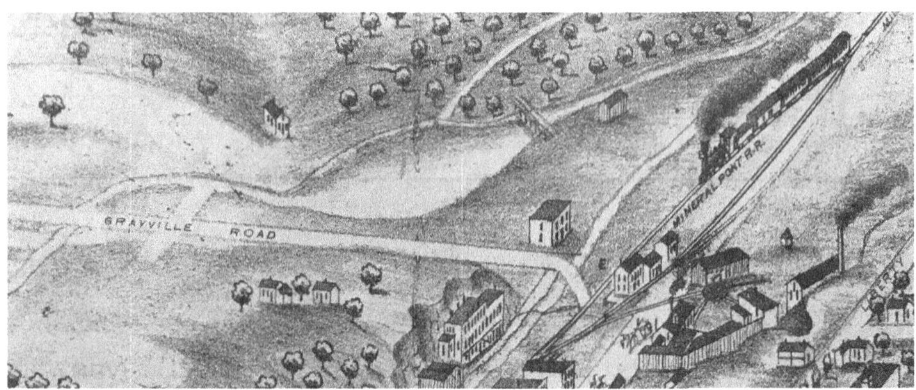

Mineral Point Historical Society

The 1864 Real Estate Assessment Roll for the City of Mineral Point indicated a building on outlot 235 with a valuation of $850. The 1867 valuation indicated buildings plural, and the valuation jumped to $900, and the 1868 valuation jumped to $2,000. It appears the warehouse was constructed beginning in 1867.

The Sam White Warehouse shown in a June 1890 photo. Mineral Point Library Archives

Sam had formed an early partnership in his grain and lumber business with a man named William Coad. The length of this partnership is unknown, but on August 4, 1870, an article in the *Mineral Point Tribune* informed the public the partnership had been dissolved.

Mineral Point Tribune, August 4, 1870

The partnership of Coad & White grain and lumber was dissolved by the death of Mr. William Coad. All persons holding claims against the late firm are notified to present them to the undersigned for adjustment. All persons indebted to said firm are notified to immediately settle their indebtedness... SAMUEL WHITE, (surviving partner)

These early electric power lines run past the Sam White Warehouse on Darlington Road, circa 1900. Mineral Point Library Archives

Some months later on March 15, 1872, Sam White and his wife, Mary Ann, who was William Coad's sister, sold an undivided 1/2 part outlot 235 to William Coad's wife, Elizabeth, and her seven children for $1.00. I think Sam and his wife, Mary Ann, were trying to help support Elizabeth and her family after William's death.

The following stories making reference to the Sam White Warehouse appeared in the *Mineral Point Tribune* papers.

Mineral Point Tribune, September 18, 1873

ACCIDENT FROM RECKLESS DRIVING

Last Thursday evening about 8 o'clock, Mrs. Wm. Jacka and her daughters, Mrs. Huxtable and Mrs. Paynter, and a child were returning in a one-horse vehicle from the country, and had got as far as the bridge between the R. R. Track and **Whites's warehouse**, when they were met by a team going at a rapid rate in the opposite direction, and the horse, little wagon, ladies and children were all thrown over the south side of the bridge in with the rocks and

> water. Assistance was soon at hand, and the ladies and children were taken up, all more or less hurt and some of them quite severely, though fortunately not fatally. The little wagon was, of course, demolished, and the horse seriously hurt. It is almost a miracle that someone was not killed.
>
> ### *Mineral Point Tribune*, August 15, 1877
>
> The warehouse of **Samuel White** in this city was burglarized last Friday night, and the safe broken open and rifled. The contents consisted of a little change—less than a dollar—books, papers, &c., all of which save the change was found scattered about the room. The tools used were taken from the railroad shop, which had first been broken into by the burglars. No clue has been obtained as to who were the perpetrators.

After William Coad's death, Sam White continued to operate his warehouse business along with buying and selling grain and lumber. In 1876, he purchased a piece of land next to the warehouse with the idea of expanding his lumber business. This land was purchased from Frank Woodman, the son of Cyrus Woodman, who originally sold the warehouse land to Sam. Details of this transaction are shown in the following abstract.

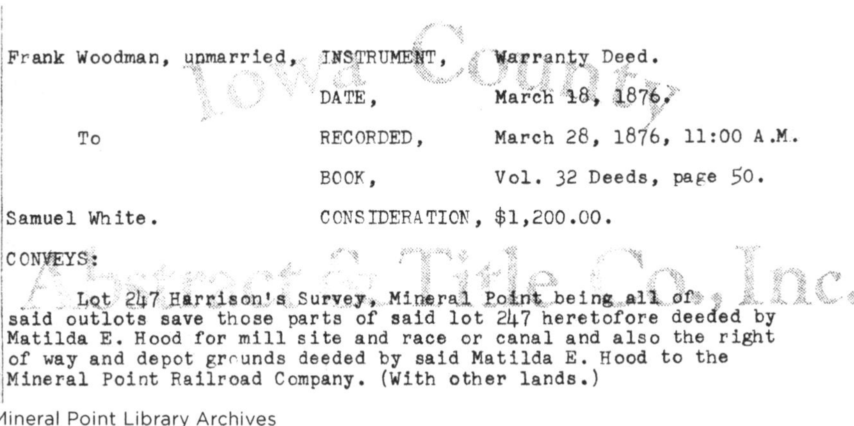

Frank Woodman, unmarried,	INSTRUMENT,	Warranty Deed.
	DATE,	March 18, 1876.
To	RECORDED,	March 28, 1876, 11:00 A.M.
	BOOK,	Vol. 32 Deeds, page 50.
Samuel White.	CONSIDERATION,	$1,200.00.

CONVEYS:

Lot 247 Harrison's Survey, Mineral Point being all of said outlots save those parts of said lot 247 heretofore deeded by Matilda E. Hood for mill site and race or canal and also the right of way and depot grounds deeded by said Matilda E. Hood to the Mineral Point Railroad Company. (With other lands.)

Mineral Point Library Archives

Sam White's Lumber Yard is shown next to the south side of his warehouse in this 1884 Sanborn map. Sam was listed as a lumber dealer in the 1880 census.

Sam White passed away on April 9, 1885. The April 10th *Iowa County Democrat* reported that he had carried on a successful business buying and selling grain and lumber and that he was a man highly respected by his friends and neighbors.

After Sam's death, the Iowa County Court assigned those

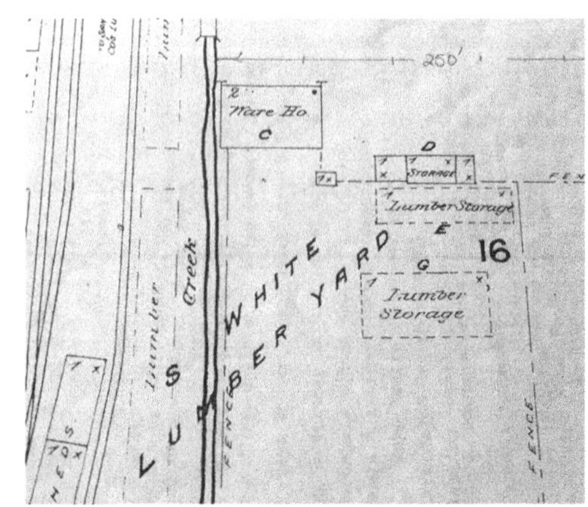

1884 Sanborn Fire Insurance Map

parts of outlots 235 and 247 to his wife, Mary Ann, and their seven children. Sam's heirs in turn sold outlot 247 to Phil Allen Jr., on June 8, 1890. Sam's son, Albion L. White, continued to operate the warehouse and lumber yard. This 1889 Sanborn Fire Insurance Map shows the **A. L. White W. HO. & Lumber Yard.**

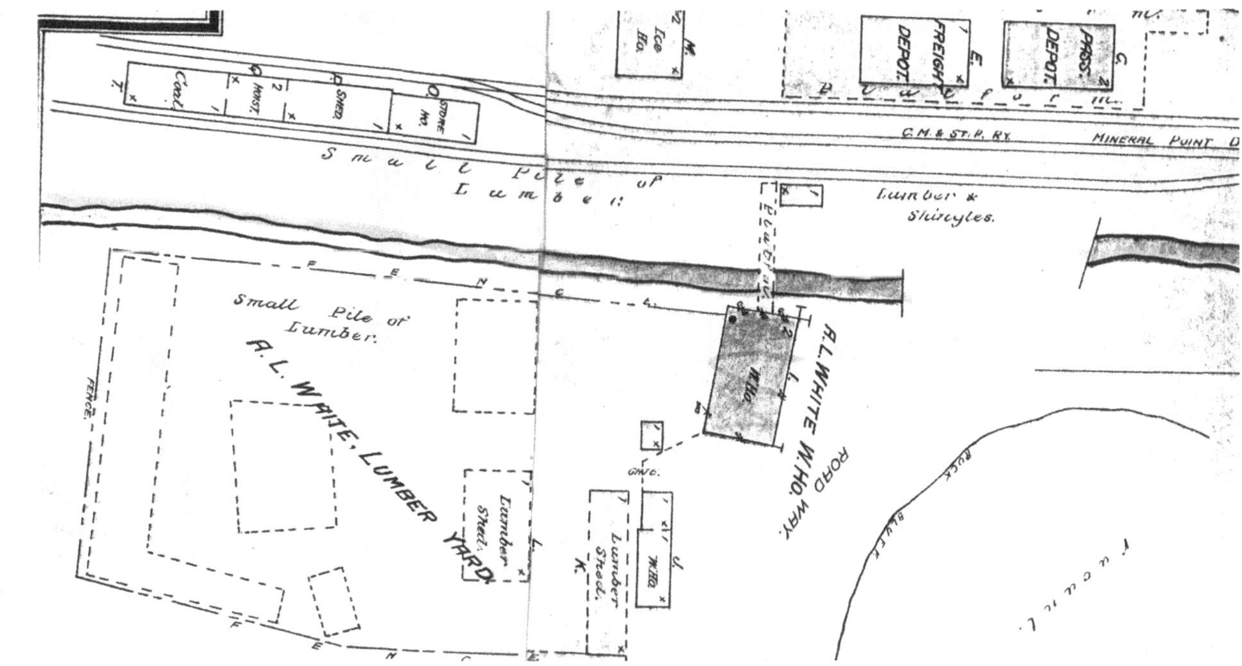

Mineral Point Library Archives

On Friday night, June 19, 1890, Mineral Point residents experienced a thunderstorm it would not soon forget. Afternoon showers turned into heavy rain, sending down torrents of water. A flood of water rushed down upon Butler's Dam, causing it to burst, releasing a wall of water resulting in heavy damage downstream. Much of White's Lumber Yard was swept away. The following account of the storm was told in the *Mineral Point Tribune.*

Mineral Point Tribune, June 19, 1890

The first indication of danger was at the depot, when water began rushing over the platform, about half past nine. Shortly after this a huge current, like unto a wall of water it is said, came rushing down the ravine east of the depot carrying everything before it. After tearing down and passing through the old Butler dam the destructive wave attacked White's lumber yard with increased force. The major part of the lumber in the yard was picked up and carried on the bosom of the water in large sections just as piled. The mad current thus freighted struck broadside of the railroad track immediately below the depot building. Ties and rails were swept clean from the bed and the hard, solid bed between the water tank and the first bridge artistically gutted. Lumber, rubbish, gravel, grass, etc. we're strewn promiscuously

This photo was taken on June 20, 1890, after a wall of water swept White's lumber inventory down the valley. Mineral Point Library Archives

> around the depot and cars standing on the tracks up as high as the body of the cars. The rushing water with its cargo of lumber continued down the course of the railroad...

After the flood, Albion White salvaged what lumber he could and continued to manage the warehouse and lumber yard for the next few years. Ads for product available at the White warehouse appeared in the *Iowa County Democrat* occasionally.

Iowa County Democrat, April 24, 1891

LIME! LIME! LIME!

One car load of lime just arrived in barrels. Cheaper than any lime. All fresh, no air slack, not exposed to air, at **White's** lumber yard.

On February 5, 1892, A. L. White placed a notice in the *Iowa County Democrat* advertising lumber at wholesale prices was available at the warehouse. Less than a year later on January 13, 1893, an announcement in the *Iowa County Democrat* told that Mr. W. A. Doy from Stillwater, Minnesota, had purchased the lumber business of A. L. White.

Iowa County Democrat, January 13, 1893

IMPORTANT ANNOUNCEMENT

Having bought out the lumber business of A. L. White, I will on or about the first of February, have one of the most complete stocks of lumber, sash, doors, etc. in fact all in the building line. Would like for you to come and see me before buying elsewhere. I can give you new material and save you money in quality and price. W. A. Doy

By the end of 1893, A. L. White was no longer involved in the lumber yard or the warehouse. The lumber yard had been mostly washed away three years earlier and was later sold. Then on December 15, 1893, a news brief announced that *John C. Martin will start up his feed mill in White's Warehouse on Monday next.*

Iowa County Democrat, December 29, 1893

FEED MILL

John C. Martin & Son have their feed mill in operation, at White's old warehouse and are prepared to do grinding in a first-class manner. They also keep feed of all kinds for sale.

Iowa County Democrat, March 16, 1894

MINERAL POINT CITY MILLS

FEED, CORN MEAL AND GRAHAM

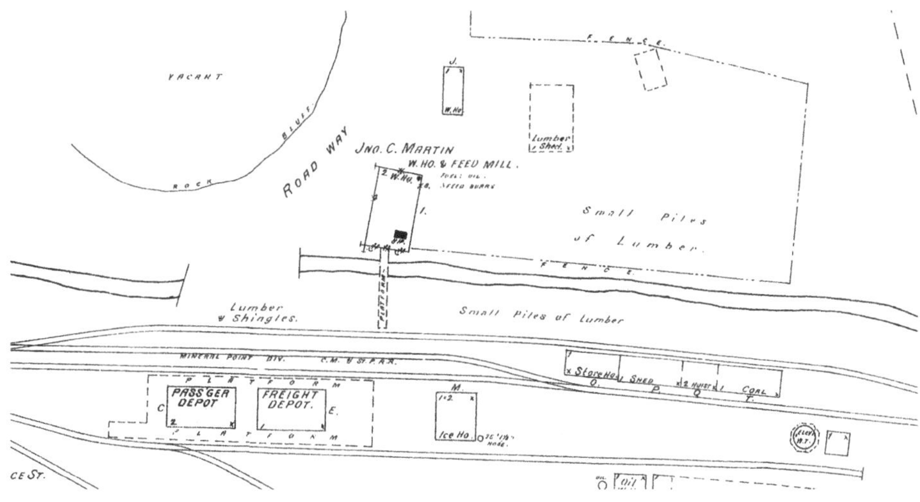

The John. C. Martin W. HO. & Feed Mill shown on the 1894 Sanborn.

We have fitted up a Mill in the stone warehouse by the railroad track, and are prepared to GRIND FEED, CORN MEAL AND GRAHAM...

Although the Whites no longer conducted business at the warehouse, the Mineral Point Real Estate Assessment Rolls show that the Samuel White and William Coad heirs continued to pay taxes on outlot 235 for several more years.

A portion of the collapsed south wall and roof of the Sam White warehouse can be seen in this June, 1911 photo.
Mineral Point Library Archives

By 1900, the Sanborn Fire Insurance Map shows the warehouse to be dilapidated and without an occupant. The 1908 and 1911 Sanborn maps also show the warehouse to be dilapidated.

Two-and-a-half years later, in an apparent dilapidated and deteriorating condition, the following ad was posted in the *Iowa County Democrat:*

Iowa County Democrat, December 25, 1913

BUY REAL ESTATE

IN A PROSPEROUS AND GROWING TOWN

The undivided one-half interest in the stone warehouse east of the railway tracks at the depot.

The 1915 Sanborn Map does not show a structure where the White warehouse once stood on Darlington Road, and the Mineral Point tax roles had no assessment for improvements in 1916, 1917, 1918 and beyond. The Sam White warehouse had vanished from the records.

After the Sam White warehouse on Darlington Road became dilapidated and uninhabitable, John Martin moved his feed store and milling business to the old Hadfield warehouse at the corner of High and Commerce Streets. This building was built by John Hadfield in 1876.

Iowa County Democrat, December 26, 1901

FLOUR AND FEED

Having purchased and refitted the large building known as the Hadfield warehouse (near corner of High and Commerce Streets, Mineral Point), I will carry a full line of flour, feed, salt, etc., and respectfully ask for a share of the trade. John C. Martin

Several years later, John Martin moved his business again and purchased a building that was referred to as the White warehouse. This reference to the White warehouse can be somewhat confusing. This was not the Darlington Road White warehouse. The building referred to in this article was actually the Penhallegan/Polkinghorn building located at 111 Commerce Street.

Iowa County Democrat, February 12, 1920

MARTIN CALF FEED COMPANY BUY BUILDING

> To accommodate their growing business the Martin Calf Feed Company have purchased from Daniel Lee what is known as the White warehouse building. It is a fine stone structure and the rear abuts on the railroad track, which makes it convenient for shipping.

The following article further clarifies the location of this new Martin Calf Feed Company that was called the White warehouse.

Iowa County Democrat, October 14, 1920

THE MARTIN CALF FEED COMPANY

> That going and growing local enterprise. The Martin Calf Feed Co. is having the large Polkinghorn store building and warehouse made over for the more convenient manufacture, sale and shipment of their good products.

Reference to the White warehouse in the February 1920 article can be explained by an examination of the Iowa County Grantor/Grantee index. In 1892, this property was purchased from James Polkinghorn on an administration deed by Jennie N. White. In 1916, Jennie N. White sold the warehouse to Daniel Lee. Daniel Lee then sold the Polkinghorn store, known as the White warehouse at this time, to the Martin Calf Feed Company as mentioned in the February, 12, 1920 *Iowa County Democrat.* Without knowing these property transactions, the purchase of the so-called White warehouse by John Martin can be confusing.

The original Sam White warehouse stood on the corner of Darlington Road, across the creek from the railroad depot for 47 years. When the Martin Calf Feed Co. moved from this large rock building, it most likely deteriorated due to neglect. The rock from this dilapidated and falling-down warehouse was probably salvaged and used in other buildings. There is no sign today of where the warehouse once stood.

There are some interesting side stories to the old Sam White warehouse and lumberyard property. In 1948, Clarence Gratz purchased this land from Iowa County. Soon afterward, Clarence dug a large pond which became known as Gratz's Pond. It was a favorite unofficial park of sorts where Mineral Pointers went to fish and skate. Clarence, with his generous ways and concern for the kids, took the wheels off an old school bus and parked it near the pond for skaters to change into their skates. Clarence later built a small warming shack near the pond, and in 1959, he installed old light posts around the pond for nighttime skating.

Gratz's Pond, circa 1950.

Clarence's son, Mike, tells an interesting story about the good old days when he was removing snow from the pond in preparation for skating. All of a sudden, the ice cracked, and his 1955 550 Oliver tractor sank to the bottom of the pond with only the exhaust pipe left showing. Mike says he stood on the hood of the tracker holding on to the exhaust pipe until he could be rescued. After being rescued, a cable was attached to the tractor's axel, and it was dragged from the pond, repaired and lived to plow again. This happened more than once, according to Mike.

Mike also tells the story of when he was mowing grass around the edge of the pond and got mired in the mud. Unable to free himself and the tractor, he looked down and was horrified to see dozens of snakes beginning to climb over the mower and up onto the tractor. Mike again climbed onto the hood of his tractor and waited to be rescued.

Gratz's Pond

There's one last story about this small piece of real estate which gained fame in Mineral Point lore long before Sam White's warehouse was built or Clarence Gratz dug his pond: A gallows had been built near here in 1842 to hang a man named William Caffee for the murder of Samuel Southwick. On November 1, 1842, William Caffee rode on his coffin to the gallows to be hanged. This was the first legal hanging in the state of Wisconsin, and November 1 became a holiday of sorts in Mineral Point. For those interested, a more detailed account of what became known as "hanging day" can be found in "The Story of Mineral Point 1827–1941."

CHAPTER 12: JOHN HADFIELD TALLOW FACTORY, 1883–1892

"1881 History of Iowa County"

JOHN HADFIELD BIOGRAPHICAL SKETCH (PG. 860)

JOHN HADFIELD, dealer in buying and shipping hides, wool, tallow and flax seed; is a native of Derbyshire, England, and was born Aug. 7, 1828. After reaching manhood, in 1850 he emigrated (sic) to the United States, and came the same year to Wisconsin, and located in Waukesha Co. In 1855, he came to Mineral Point, and the same year began buying hides; has continued in the business since then for a period of twenty-five years, and has transacted a large and successful business. He is the largest dealer and shipper of hides in this section of the state; also deals extensively in wool, tallow and flax-seed. He has built up an enviable reputation for honesty, integrity and fair dealing, and "his word is his bond." Mr. Hadfield married Mary H. Collins from Devonshire, England; she died June 29, 1873, leaving three children—Frank W., John A., and Mary E. On the 5th of August, 1874, Mr. Hadfield was united in marriage to Mary Rogers, a native of Cornwall, England; they have three children—Sallie R., Emily G., and an infant son.

Soon after arriving in Mineral Point, Hadfield began buying, selling and shipping hides. He also opened a boot and shoe manufacturing shop on High Street across from the courthouse. The following ad appeared in the May 30, 1855 *Mineral Point Tribune*.

***Mineral Point Tribune*, May 30, 1855**

New Boot and Shoe Shop.

THE subscriber has just opened a **BOOT and SHOE SHOP** in the room recently occupied as the office of the Mineral Point Democrat, nearly opposite the Court House, where he is prepared, with first quality Stock and the best of Workmen, to manufacture, on short notice, all kinds of

BOOTS & SHOES,

in the best manner, and on reasonable terms, and Warranted to be equal to any work done in the State. The public are invited to call, and ascertain for themselves, his prices and the appearance of his work. Feeling confident that he can satisfy all who are in want of **Boots and Shoes**, he would respectfully solicit a share of public patronage.

JOHN HADFIELD.

Mineral Point, March 16, 1855. 6m18.

In 1857, Hadfield advertised the finest and best leather assortment ever brought from the East to Mineral Point, which he could manufacture into boots and shoes on short notice. He had French Cork Soles to prevent cold feet, and he advertised a leather preservative which would supersede every other article of its kind, wherever its qualities are known.

Along with operating his boot and shoe store, Hadfield continued buying and selling buffalo robes, cow hides, sheep skins and wool for many years, and *he was known far and wide as an active, honorable business man.*

On March 24, 1883, John Hadfield bought from Samuel White for $100.00 a small plot of land on Darlington Road just east of the Mineral Point Railroad Depot. A description of this land reads as follows:

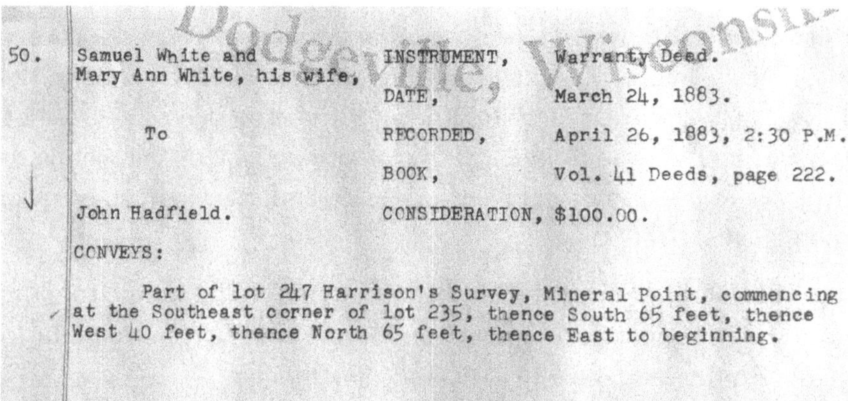

50. Samuel White and Mary Ann White, his wife,

To

John Hadfield.

INSTRUMENT,	Warranty Deed.
DATE,	March 24, 1883.
RECORDED,	April 26, 1883, 2:30 P.M.
BOOK,	Vol. 41 Deeds, page 222.
CONSIDERATION,	$100.00.

CONVEYS:

Part of lot 247 Harrison's Survey, Mineral Point, commencing at the Southeast corner of lot 235, thence South 65 feet, thence West 40 feet, thence North 65 feet, thence East to beginning.

Hadfield had plans to build a plant for the rendering of tallow and the production of neatsfoot oil.

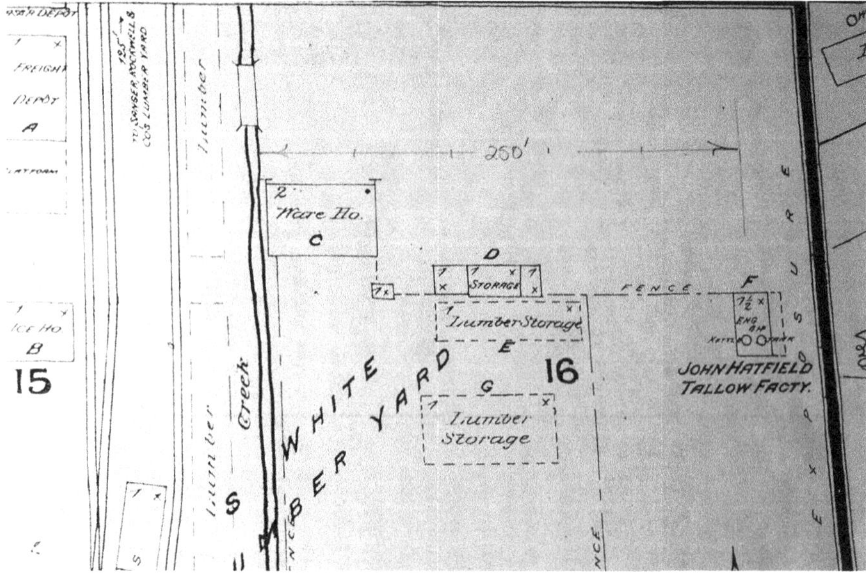

1884 Sandborn Fire Insurance Map Mineral Point Library Archives

The square on this 2020 aerial shows where the tallow factory was located.

Iowa County Democrat, April 13, 1883

RENDERING ESTABLISHMENT

ONE MORE ENTERPRISE SUCCESSFULLY CARRIED ON IN MINERAL POINT

On Tuesday last a reporter of The Democrat visited the Rendering establishment of John Hadfield, near the depot in this city. The building is a two-story frame, 18x32 feet, with large boiler, (Gate City Steam Generator No. 2), on the first floor, and a large tank, capacity 500 gallons, reaching from the first floor up through to the second floor of the building where it is "loaded" or filled with rough tallow, for rendering. About a ton of tallow is usually placed in the tank at a time, when the steam arrangements from the boiler are attached to the tank and the rendering process begins. Mr. Hadfield informed the Democrat man that he can render three tanks of tallow per week, being from twelve hundred to fifteen hundred gallons.

The work of the establishment is not confined to the rendering of tallow alone, but to the obtaining of neatfoot oil by boiling the feet of slaughtered oxen, cows and calves; and to the calcining of bones.

Mr. Hadfield feels confident that the enterprise will prove a paying one. He buys rough tallow, butchers' bones and dry bones and animals' feet, and bones of all kinds. He intends to keep the establishment running to its full capacity. Small boys may be seen with wheelbarrows full of bones going to Mr. Hadfield's warehouse or to the rendering establishment. These bones are shipped by car load to be used for fertilizing purposes. The rough tallow is obtained from our butchers here and from neighboring towns.

> Mr. Hadfield has invested quite a sum of money in the lot, building and fixtures, and is entitled to credit for the enterprise which he has shown is furnishing a market at home for all the surplus tallow, and bones within a radius of twenty or thirty miles.

The warehouse mentioned in the above article was located at 22 High Street in Mineral Point. It was a multi-purpose 25x80-foot, two-story stone building for warehousing raw materials and supplies for the tallow factory, plus it had rooms suitable for a store and other places of business.

The building of the warehouse was announced in the following article.

Mineral Point Tribune, August 12, 1875

> Mr. Hadfield is preparing to erect a large building near the corner of High and Commerce Streets, to be occupied as a warehouse, and which will also contain rooms suitable for a store or other places of business. The building will be erected of stone, with an area of 25x80 feet, and will be two stories high. It will be finished early in the spring.

Iowa County Democrat, April 19, 1876

> Mr. Hadfield is pushing work on his new building (warehouse) and will have it ready for occupancy this fall. A magnificent hall is to be fitted up in the second story for the Good Templars, and will be furnished elegantly.

The building that John Hadfield built at 22 High Street in 1876 is shown below. It was built as a warehouse for raw materials and supplies for his tallow factory. In addition, it had space for a store and other places of business.

John Sharp 2021.

Hadfield's business interests were many. Not only did he buy and sell hides, have a shoe and boot store and a rendering plant, but several articles describing his dealings in lime, coal and Washburn Gold Medal Flour appeared in the Mineral Point papers over the years, and after retirement, if he ever did retire, he became landlord of the Gate House in Platteville, Wisconsin, which he owned. (wisconsinhistory.org #46471)

Other stories of interest related to John Hadfield were printed in Mineral Point papers.

Mineral Point Tribune, August 6, 1874

Runaway.—In proceeding to the residence of his bride, in Willow Springs, yesterday morning, Mr. John Hadfield met with an accident; his fine carriage was upset, horses ran away, and the carriage badly shattered. Mr. H. fortunately escaped unhurt, and was on hand in time to get married and with his bride took the 6 o'clock train for New York.

Willow Springs was the residence of Mary Rogers who Mr. Hadfield married after his first wife, Mary H. Collins, passed away.

Iowa County Democrat, April 4, 1884

John Hadfield has just received a car load of the famous Waukesha lime.

Iowa County Democrat, May 2, 1890

John Hadfield shipped from Mineral Point since the first of last December, nearly $60,000 worth of hides, pelts and rendered tallow. Can any shipper in Wisconsin make as big a showing? And yet there are many who think Mineral Point is not much of a town for business.

Iowa County Democrat, July 24, 1891

COAL! COAL!

We are making very low prices on Coal, for July and August delivery. Call and see me before buying. John Hadfield

Iowa County Democrat, February 19, 1892

Just received by John Hadfield, a car load of Washburn Gold Medal Flour—the best in the world. Try it. Every sack warranted.

The Mineral Point City (grist) Mill was no longer operational as a mill in 1892, and Hadfield, being the astute business man he was, was filling the need for baking flour in Mineral Point and surrounding areas.

Iowa County Democrat, February 19, 1892

A LARGE PURCHASE OF HIDES

THE LANCASTER HERALD

J. A. Hadfield, the hide buyer of Mineral Point, bought of Joe Nathan & Son, last week, 750 beef hides, probably the largest lot of hides ever sold by any one firm in this city before. Nathan & Son have a vat in which the hides are salted and stored, thus preventing any possibility of their spoiling.

Iowa County Democrat, April 1, 1892

The Platteville Witness: John Hadfield has assumed personal charge of the Gate House, and will make a popular landlord. His family has arrived and are now at home to the public.

Iowa County Democrat, September 2, 1892

John Hadfield has retired from business and is succeeded by N. Brewer & Co. The members of the new firm are all straight, substantial and enterprising men, and will so conduct the business as to hold the large trade enjoyed by Mr. Hadfield, and will increase it if possible. The Democrat wishes them success.

On September 9, 1892, John and Mary Hadfield sold by warranty deed to Phillip Allen Jr. for $50, the plot of land along Darlington Road where the Hadfield Tallow Factory was located (Vol. 57 Deeds, page 378, 1893).

The tallow business was carried on by N. Brewer & Company.

Iowa County Democrat, September 16, 1892

SPECIAL ANNOUNCEMENT

Having succeeded Mr. Hadfield we are pleased to announce that we shall carry a full stock of flour, all kinds of feed, and salt. Our prices will be the lowest. We handle Washburn, Crosby & Co.'s, "Gold Medal" flour, and will use special delivery wagon for flour and feed. N. Brewer & Co.

Mineral Point Tribune, September 17, 1892

Having succeeded Mr. John Hadfield, we desire to announce that in addition to the hide and tallow business, we shall carry a full stock of flour, feed, salt, etc. which we will deliver by special delivery wagon to any part of the city.

Washburn, Crosby & Co's, famous "Gold Medal" flour always on hand. N. Brewer & Co.

Iowa County Democrat, November 17, 1893

JOHN HADFIELD

Early on Friday morning Nov. 10th, Mr. John Hadfield, one of Mineral Point's most highly respected citizens, fell asleep in death, after a painful illness of many months. His wife, four sons and four daughters survive him...

He was known far and wide as an active, honorable business man. During his residence here of thirty-eight years he was brought into business relations with the whole people of southern Wisconsin, by whom his word was ever regarded as good as his bond...

The large church was filled to overflowing with citizens who had come to pay their last tribute of respect to the memory of the deceased. The body was laid to rest in Graceland cemetery.

CHAPTER 13: EARLY 1900S ON DARLINGTON ROAD

In the early 1900s, three new businesses started along the south side of Darlington Road east of the railroad depot. They were located on small parcels of land right next to one another, and each parcel was purchased from R. G. White, his wife, Mary, and L. A. Ross. All of these businesses and the land parcels they were located on have interesting and varied histories. The first to be established was the Mineral Point Concrete Construction Company, which began in 1909. Then came the Winona Oil Company in 1920, and finally the Mineral Point Oil Company in 1924. At some time during the late 1920s and 1930s, a small Standard Oil service station was built on parcel #1 and was operated by a local family.

The dot in triangle #1 indicates the location of a Standard Oil filling station.

Parcel #1

MINERAL POINT CONCRETE CONSTRUCTION COMPANY 1909 to 1921

R. G. & Mary White & L. A. Ross to M. P. Concrete Const. Co., May 16, 1910. Consideration $50.00

(Quit Claim Deed. Vol. 77 Deeds, page 236)

Parcel #2

WINONA OIL COMPANY 1920 to 1940

R. G. & Mary White & L. A. Ross to Winona Oil Company, June 3, 1920. Consideration $400.00

(Warranty Deed. Vol. 103 Deeds, page 248)

Parcel #3

MINERAL POINT OIL COMPANY 1924 to 1976

R. G. & Mary White & L. A. Ross to Mineral Point Oil Company,

May 3,1924. Consideration $532.00

(Warranty Deed. Vol. 107 Deeds, page 399)

Parcel #1 Mineral Point Concrete Construction Company

The Mineral Point Concrete Construction Company was organized on September 17, 1909, and was the first of these three companies to purchase land along Darlington Road on May 16, 1910. The company conducted a prosperous concrete construction business until June 2, 1921, when a dynamite explosion destroyed the factory building and its equipment. The company did not recover from this accident and was not rebuilt. (Its history will be discussed at length in its own chapter.)

After the concrete plant exploded in 1921, the property was turned into a junk yard and salvage business. There is a debate about who collected the first pile of junk here, Sam Mead or Jake Gordon? Information on the early years of the junk yard business is scarce. Whoever it was, they started a business that continued for 68 years and had three different owners and a very large presence along Darlington Road. Every gear head and person hunting a car part or piece of iron came from near and far to the yard, including myself.

The first bit of information I could find about the junk yard appeared in the *Iowa County Democrat,* and I'm not sure if there is a connection between the L. Mead named in this article and Sam Mead.

Iowa County Democrat, November 30, 1922

JUNK BOUGHT

We are buying all kinds of junk, fur and hides. L. Mead

The only other related information I could find appeared in the M. P. City Government minutes in 1937.

The Democrat, June 21, 1937

CITY GOVERNMENT

The License Committee recommends the granting of a junk dealers' license to Jake Gordon. Motion made by Alderman Mauger, seconded by Alderman Stevens that the license be granted. Motion carried by following vote: Aye: Jeuck, Mauger, Stevens, Markgraf, Ralph and Grange. No: Schimming.

Jake Gordon Junkyard

Not having any definitive information about who actually started the junk yard, Jake Gordon seems to be a likely choice since I was able to get some information about the yard talking to local resident, Paul Whitford.

Paul grew up in Mineral Point, and in a sidewalk conversation with Paul on March 7, 2009, Paul remembers as a six-year-old boy in 1936 how a yard man named "Dude Young" lived in the old gas station when Jake Gordon ran the yard. Dude got the name Dude because he always dressed up fancy and wore spats when he came to town on Saturday night.

Paul also recalled how he and his buddies would pick up scrap iron that had spilled by the tracks near the depot and then sell it to Jake. Jake finally told the boys the iron had his metal shear marks on it, and he couldn't keep buying it from them since he'd already bought it once from someone else.

The old gas station Paul talked about was a Standard Oil filling station operated by the Joe Filardo family. This station pumped gas from the late 1920s into the 1930s and was built along Darlington Road on the junk yard. At that time, Darlington Road was the main road into Mineral Point from the east. Several Mineral Pointers talk of stopping at the station for 25-cents-a-gallon gas as they left town on their way to Darlington.

Standard Oil Filling Station

I was fortunate enough to have had a telephone conversation with Rose Filardo Temple, Joe's daughter, on April 12, 2014, just before her 100th birthday. Rose told me her father, Joe Filardo, and her uncle, Joe Garcia, ran this filling station on the old cement plant property along Darlington Road in the late 1920s and 1930s. Rose remembered the station was a two-pump Standard Oil station, and the pump with a "Red Crown" globe on its top pumped premium gas, and the pump with the "White Crown" globe on its top pumped regular gas.

The Filardos lived on the south side of town, and Rose recalled how she delivered sack lunches to her father and Uncle Joe by walking along the railroad tracks past the large rubber plant chimney, over the railroad bridge and on to the station. Rose said her brothers Frank, Nick, Bruno, Joe and Dominic all worked at the station, and that "Crazy Joe" and his friend, Frank Bertuci, both claimed to have pumped gas for John Dillinger while working there.

Red Crown glass Pump Top

White Crown glass Pump Top

The arrow in this circa 1927 aerial photo points to the filling station. Wisconsin State Historical Society

This 1998 photo shows the remains of the old Standard Oil service station on Darlington Road. Photo courtesy of Paul Wagner, Darlington Wisconsin.

Dave Fine Salvage Yard

In 1940, Dave Fine came to Mineral Point from Milwaukee and bought the junk yard business from Jake Gordon. Dave owned and operated the yard for the next 27 years.

Four years after buying the salvage yard business from Jake Gordon, Dave bought the old concrete company land from Elizabeth and Norman Kieffer for $600 on October 20, 1944. Parcel #1 below. (Warranty Deed. Vol. 156 Deeds, page 321)

Three years later in 1947, Dave expanded the junk yard by purchasing land from Clarence and Betsy Gratz for $450. Parcel #2 below. (Warranty Deed. Vol. 158 Deeds, page 284)

This aerial photograph shows the parcels owned by Dave Fine in 1947.

In a phone conversation with Dave Fine's son Paul in February 2009, Paul recounted the memories he had about the salvage yard.

> *Dad bought the salvage yard business from Jake Gordon in the fall of 1940. We moved to Mineral Point the next spring and lived on Doty Street. We later moved to 402 Maiden. The Harkers lived on one side, and the Meads lived on the other.*
>
> *The yard dealt in cast iron, steel and other metals, and it was the only scrap yard between Platteville and Madison.*
>
> *Scrap iron was loaded into train cars that came to the yard on the old zinc works spur. When the spur was discontinued in 1946/47, Dad bid on and got the salvage rights to remove the bridge over the creek and the track on the east side of the bridge. After removing the track, he then leveled the train road bed on the east side of the stream to make more salvage yard area. Scrap iron was then hauled down to the depot and loaded on trains cars there.*

The old gas station was used as yard headquarters and a change room for the men. We stored brass and copper in the station, and a metal shear was kept in there. Dad bought cow and horse hides, mink, muskrat and fox. Trapping was big back then. The smaller skins were stretched with welding rod, hung in the station to dry and then sold when enough had been collected.

Dad later moved yard headquarters into a building on Commerce Street (203 Commerce Street). He sold new and used auto parts there and had all kinds of parts for old cars. He did welding and had an oxygen truck he kept there. Winfred Mosley worked in the store and cut flat glass for the old cars and trucks before rounded glass came in 1953. Dad also bought rags and paper from boys who collected it during the war.

Dad also remembered how Jim Johnson and Francis Basting would pick scrap iron up along the railroad tracks in wheelbarrows and then bring it to the scrap yard and sell it to earn enough cash to buy suits for high school graduation. This was in about 1947. They each bought suits from Frances Stude's clothing store for $17.00. In 1948, when the new highway

This circa 1944 photo shows young Jim Jungbluth in front of Dave Fine's Commerce Street "Point Auto Wreckers" business with a goat wagon full of waste paper he had collected for the war effort.
Photo courtesy of Ruth Jungbluth.

was built, the road builders hit a lead vein when making the big cut through Merry Christmas Hill. People from all over town rushed to pick up pieces of lead and then brought it to the yard and sold it to Dad for cash. Jim Johnson's older brother, Norm, bought a 1936 Ford Coupe in 1943 that had a clutch problem. Norm and Keith Mitchell lifted the hood on that old Ford and put a new clutch in.

In 1967, Dave sold the junk yard on land contract to Melbourne and Charleen Johnston and Edwin and Cheryl Richards, a partnership, doing business as E and M Salvage and Scrap Yards. In 1968, the Johnstons and the Richards transferred ownership of the land by land contract to Keith Mitchell, and in 1973, the Johnstons sold the land by quitclaim deed to Keith D. Mitchell and his wife, Kathryn, for $2,750 (Quit Claim Deed, Vol. 286, page 229). This was the start of the Keith Mitchell Salvage Yard.

Keith Mitchell Salvage Yard

The Mitchell Salvage Yard was in operation from 1968 to 1984. By 1984, the yard had expanded to cover the land between Old Darlington Road and Mineral Point Creek as indicated by the black line shown on page 116.

In 1984, Keith had the old cars and other metal crushed and hauled away before selling the property to Ted Landon. In 1997, Jennifer and John Sharp bought the east end of the old salvage yard from Ted and restored it to its original condition.

Ted Landon oil painting of the Keith Mitchell Salvage Yard, circa 1980. Painting courtesy of Joel and Nina Duncanson.

This aerial photograph shows the parcels owned by Keith Mitchell in 1974.

Keith Mitchell Salvage Yard circa 1980.

The last of the Keith Mitchell Salvage Yard buildings were torn down in 2009.

John Sharp 2009

John Sharp 2009

For many gear heads and do-it-yourselfers, the junk yard was the most interesting business operation in Mineral Point. If you needed a car part, a truck part, a part for your washing machine or most any other kind of part, the salvage yard was your first stop to try and find what you needed. When Jennifer and I were restoring our gallery at 207 Commerce Street, I found all the heat duct needed to install our forced air heating system. Over the years, there were many good finds.

Parcel #2 Winona Oil Company

The WINONA OIL COMPANY bought a parcel of land along Darlington Road in 1920, and by 1921, they had constructed a metal warehouse on this land just west of the Mineral Point Concrete Construction Company. This building would later be sold to Chad Harker in 1940 and become the Chad Harker Stock Yard. Before building this warehouse, the Winona Oil Company had installed two large above-ground fuel tanks east of the concrete company where they could receive large deliveries of petroleum products from railroad tank cars.

The photo on the left (circa 1918) shows the Winona Oil Company's storage tanks east of the Mineral Point cement plant. The photo on the right shows the original Winona Oil Company warehouse which became a stock yard in 1940. The building was owned by the National Farmers Organization when this photo was taken, circa 1972.

Billy Gilman Collection, Mineral Point Library Archives

Photo courtesy of Ted Landon

The Winona Oil Company's storage tanks are shown east of the Mineral Point Concrete Construction Company on this 1916 Chicago, Milwaukee & St. Paul Railroad station map.

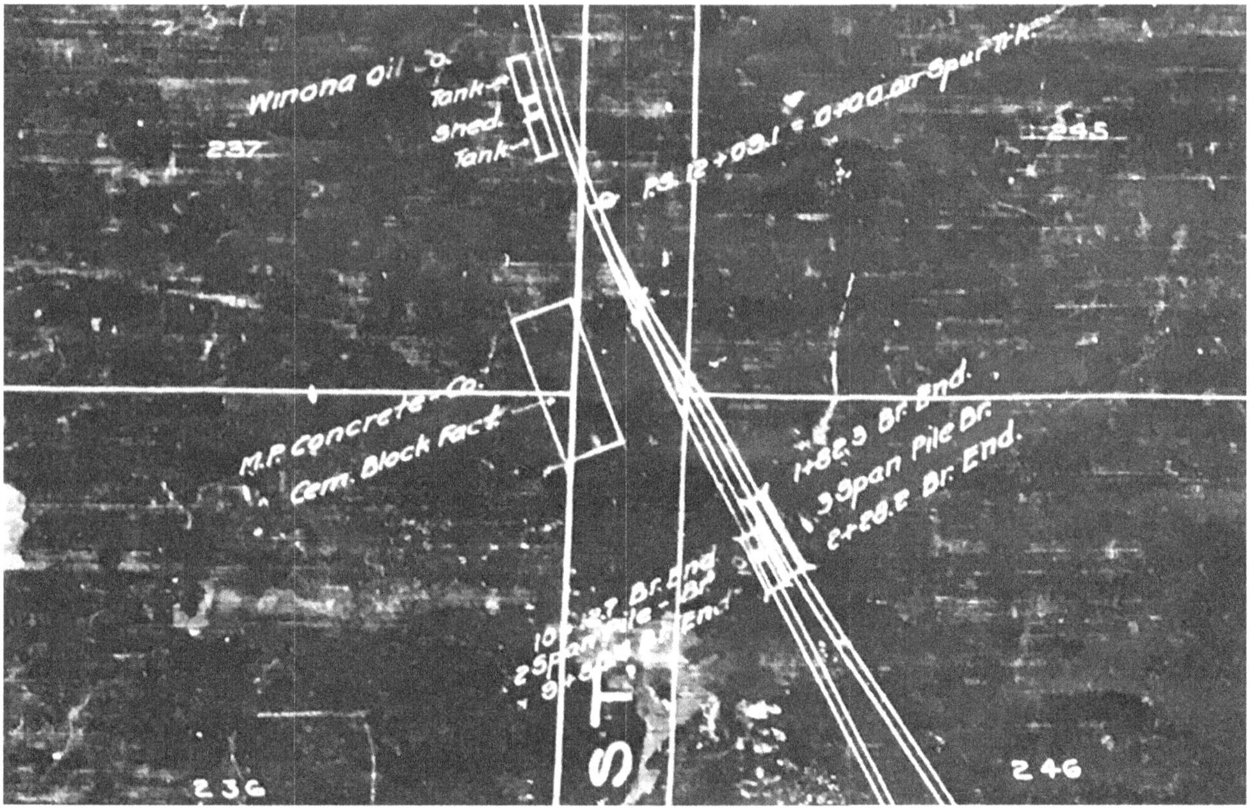

The top arrow in this 1927 arial photo points to the location of the Winona Oil Company's petroleum storage tanks along the Mineral Point and Northern Railroad spur. The bottom arrow points to the Winona Oil Company's metal warehouse.

The following article appeared in the 1928 *Iowa County Democrat*:

> ***Iowa County Democrat*, January 12, 1928**
>
> **JOHN FERRELL PURCHASES THE LOCAL WINONA OIL AGENCY**
>
> John Ferrell, who is preparing to sell his stock on his farm four and one-half miles east of Waldwick and to rent the land and out buildings, has purchased the local agency of the Winona Oil company from Gerald Salmon.
>
> Mr. Ferrell will handle gasoline, kerosene, and all kinds of cylinder oil and greases. He has purchased a new Dodge-Graham one and one-half ton truck from P. O. Vivian and is prepared to make large and small deliveries.

The 1927 one-and one-half ton Dodge-Graham truck John Ferrell purchased was probably very similar to the one shown on the cover of this June 18, 1927 Saturday Evening Post.

The Winona Oil Agency changed hands over its 20-year history. The last owner was Cities Service Oil Company, and on July 1, 1940, they sold the buildings and property to Chad Harker, and it became the Chad Harker Stock Yard (Quit Claim Deed, Vol. 134 , Deeds, page 389).

Chad Harker Stock Yard

When Chad Harker bought the old Winona Oil Company warehouse on Darlington Road, his plan was to have a small stock yard where cattle and hogs could be bought and sold. He added lean-tos to the warehouse building and built some corrals out back where livestock could be kept for short periods of time. Farmers and individuals who wanted to buy or sell a few animals could do so at Chad's corrals. On pre-planned days, farmers would bring small numbers of livestock together in preparation for shipping to market. When enough animals were gathered for shipping, they would be loaded onto stock trucks and transported to auctions in Chicago, Milwaukee or Madison.

Photo courtesy of Ted Landon

The building in the above photo (circa 1972) was the original Winona Oil Company warehouse that was built circa 1921. Chad Harker bought the property on July 1, 1940, added some corrals and lean-tos to the building, and it became known as the Chad Harker Stock Yard (Quit Claim Deed, Vol.134, Deeds, page 389). Chad operated the stock yard for the next fourteen years.

This drawing is from Alan Tucker's surveyor's book—1936/1939. It shows the property survey that was done when Chad Harker bought land from Cities Service Oil Company in 1940.

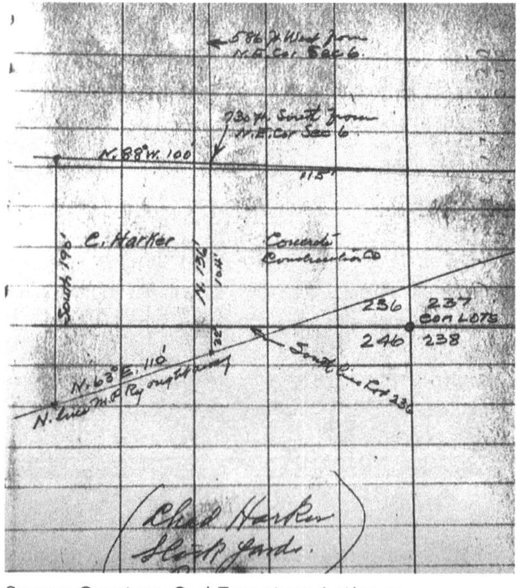

Survey Courtesy Carl Tunestam Antiques

In one of my many sidewalk conversations with Paul Whitford, Paul told me about the days in 1946 when he drove stock trucks full of cattle and hogs from Mineral Point to the Milwaukee and Chicago auctions for the Ross Brothers Trucking Company.

> *Driving a stock truck full of cattle weighing 40,000 pounds was a challenge, especially in the winter when the temperatures were below zero on some days. Beef was selling at 16 cents a pound tops, and hogs were 11 cents a pound.*

Chad sold the stock yard to Peter and Stella Trace on May 8, 1954. They kept the property for only one year and then sold it to Cecil Flanagan on October 20, 1955. Flanagan ran the pens for nine years before selling it to the National Farmers Organization in 1964. The NFO owned the stock pens for the next 20 years, and during this time, they enlarged and improved the facility. On February 23, 1984, the NFO sold the property to Harry Flanagan, Cecil's son. After operating the pens for 24 more years, Harry sold the property to Jay and Diane Homan in 2008. The Homans demolished the stock yard building and corrals and built a car port as part of their residence.

Ross Brothers stock truck pictures. Photos courtesy of Larry Ross

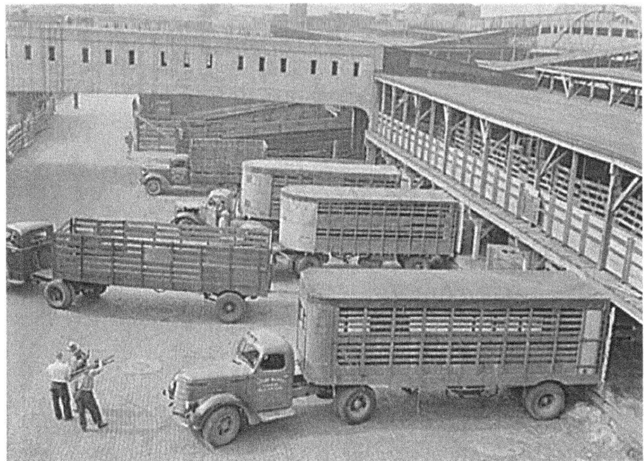

1940 stock trucks at the Union Stock Yards, Chicago, Illinois.

The above picture shows the improvements made by the NFO to the stock yard building. John Sharp 2000

Parcel #3 Mineral Point Oil Company

The Mineral Point Oil Company was organized on March 7, 1924. The Articles of Organization are recorded at the Iowa County Recorder's Office—Vol. 88 Deeds, page 143-146. They are as follows:

> Know all men by these presents: That the undersigned adult residents of the State of Wisconsin do hereby make, sign and agree to the following:
>
> ### Articles of Organization
>
> ### Article 1.
>
> The undersigned have associated and do hereby associate themselves together for the purpose of forming a Corporation under Chapters 180 to 184 inclusive, Revised Statutes of Wisconsin 1923 and the acts amendatory thereof and supplemental thereto, the business and purpose of which Corporation shall be the wholesaling and retailing of gas, kerosene, lubricating oils, greases and other oil products, which business is to be carried on within the State of Wisconsin and especially within the County of Iowa in said State.

Article 2.
The name of the Corporation shall be the Mineral Point Oil Company and its location and principal office for conduct of its business shall be 38 High Street, Mineral Point, Iowa County, Wisconsin.

Article 3.
The Capitol stock of said Corporation shall be $15,000.00 and the same shall consist of 150 shares of common stock each of which said shares shall be of the face or par value of $100.00.

Article 4.
The general officers of said corporation shall be a President, Vice President, Secretary and Treasurer. The Board of Directors shall consist of 5 stock holders.

Article 5. Duties of officers.

Articles 6 to 12. (other details)

Article 13. (other details)

The names and residence of the persons forming this Corporation are: Joseph J. Fiedler, A. F. Bishop Jr. and James P. Hutchison, all of Mineral Point, Wisconsin.

In addition to an office at 38 High Street, the Mineral Point Oil Company built a warehouse on Darlington Road where it could receive, store and distribute petroleum products to customers. This warehouse was located on the west side of the stock yards. 50 yards behind the warehouse there were several 1,200-gallon storage tanks next to the Mineral Point and Northern Zinc Company Railroad spur. The company could receive deliveries of bulk petroleum products from railroad tank cars there and then pipe it above ground to the warehouse on Darlington Road. Gas, kerosene and other oil products could then be loaded into trucks for delivery to farms, gas stations and other customers.

This 1972 photo shows the old Mineral Point Oil Company warehouse on Darlington Road.
Photo courtesy Ted Landon

Looking up Darlington Road to the M. P. Oil Company warehouse and the NFO stock pens. Photo courtesy Ted Landon

The aerial photograph above shows the bulk storage tanks along the Mineral Point and Northern Rail spur and the raised supply lines from the tanks to the Mineral Point Oil Company warehouse on Darlington Road, circa 1961.

Also seen in the photo, starting on the far left, a sliver of the Dave Fine Junk Yard, the Cecil Flanagan Livestock pens, the Mineral Point Oil Company warehouse, Gratz's Pond (dug by Clarence Gratz in 1957), the old rubber plant chimney, top center, and the main railroad right-of-way into Mineral Point.

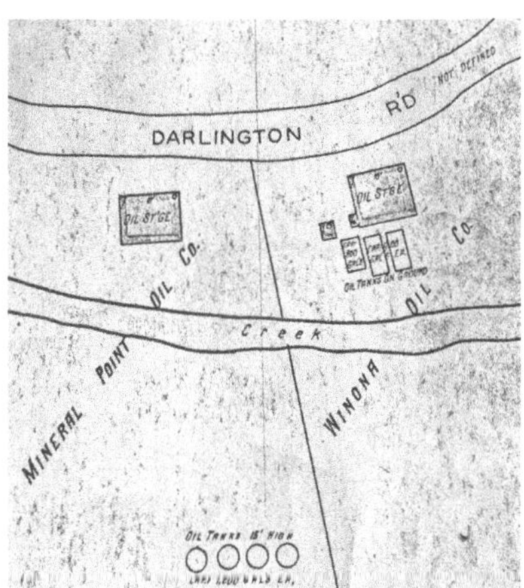

Mineral Point Library Archives

This 1929 Sanborn Insurance map shows the Mineral Point Oil Company warehouse along Darlington Road and the 1,200-gallon storage tanks located along the zinc company railroad spur. Petroleum products were off loaded into the storage tanks from railroad tank cars and then piped above ground to the warehouse on Darlington Road.

Iowa County Democrat, January 2, 1930

OIL COMPANY HOLDS MEETING

LOCALLY OWNED CORPORATION HAS VERY SUCCESSFUL YEAR; ELECT OFFICERS

The Mineral Point Oil Company, one of Mineral Point's few locally owned corporations, held its annual meeting Monday evening. The board of directors elected for this year are J. J. Fiedler, D. C. Jacka, A. F. Bishop, Jr., R. J. Gallagher and R. W. Parkinson. The directors met and elected the following officers for the ensuing year. D. C. Jacka, President; R. J. Gallagher, Vice President; R. W. Parkinson, secretary and treasurer.

The company enjoyed their most successful year since organized six years ago. They are grateful for the fine patronage that they have received from the city and surrounding vicinity.

> The company handled a total of two hundred and twenty-five thousand gallons of gasoline and kerosene and 5000 gallons of lubricating oil during the past year.
>
> The company owns two filling stations in the city and in addition have five pumps located at garages in the city. Pumps are also located at Linden, Hollandale, and Waldwick. In addition to the trade from pumps the company has enjoyed a fine bulk trade to farmers and buyers in the city and surrounding villages.
>
> D. C. Jacka, manager of the company, attributes this fine business to the fact that they handle the best grade of gasoline and kerosene and oils that can be purchased.

On December 28, 1945, the Mineral Point Oil Company was sold to the Socony-Vacuum Oil Company, a corporation duly organized and existing under and by virtue of the laws of the State of New York, and duly licensed to transact business in the State of Wisconsin. Socony-Vacuum Oil Company changed its name to Socony Mobil Oil Company on April 29, 1955, and on May 18, 1966, the name of the company was again changed and it became the **Mobil Oil Corporation.**

Local Mineral Point resident Jerry Walsh, who was discharged from the United States Navy in 1955, returned to Mineral Point and became the agent and local distributor for Socony Mobil Oil Company products in 1957. Jerry worked out of the Darlington Road Mobil Oil facilities until 1976, when the DNR closed his Darlington Road operation due to environmental concerns over its proximity to Mineral Point Creek. Jerry continued to supply petroleum products to his customers from the Clarence Springer and Goony Fisher facility south of the depot until 2004. After being in the oil business for 47 years, Jerry retired and sold his customer list to Mineral Point businessman Terry Poad that same year. Terry continues to carry Mobil Oil products at his station located at 1045 Branger Drive, Mineral Point.

John Sharp 2021

Terry Poad's Mobil Oil Station and Convenience Store located at 1045 Branger Drive, Mineral Point, Wisconsin.

On July 15, 1976, the Mobil Oil Corporation sold the Darlington Road warehouse and property to Ted Landon. Ted demolished the metal structure and built a rock addition to his residence (Quit Claim Deed, Vol. 314, page 48).

CHAPTER 14: MINERAL POINT CONCRETE CONSTRUCTION COMPANY, 1909–1921

Concrete and concrete products were becoming increasingly important as a building material in all types of construction in the first half of the 20th century. It was used more frequently on the farm for floors, foundations, posts and sidewalks and to build basements, houses, garages, barns and silos.

One of the main reasons concrete and concrete products were becoming more widely used in the U.S. was the establishment of a Portland cement industry in the late 19th century. Portland cement is a major component in concrete, and along with the wide availability of sand and gravel, it became an affordable alternative to quarried stone. In addition to the establishment of the Portland cement industry, advancements in machinery to form concrete block as a building material were being invented. In 1900, Harmon P. Palmer created a machine that combined forming and texturing of rock-faced concrete blocks. The combination of these advancements led to concrete and concrete block being advertised as a do-it-yourself, inexpensive type of building material that didn't burn, didn't decay and saved construction time.

Besides introducing hamburgers, peanut butter and ice cream cones, the 1904 St. Louis World's Fair promoted and marketed concrete as the new building material. Many of the buildings at the fair were constructed with concrete block. Thousands of people from all over the world, including Mineral Point, traveled to St. Louis to view all the newest building innovations available to the world. The weekly local news columns in the 1904 Mineral Point papers listed people who were coming and going to the fair, and the Chicago, Milwaukee & St. Paul Railway advertised special rates from the Mineral Point Railroad Depot to the St. Louis World's Fair.

***Iowa County Democrat*, September 22, 1904**

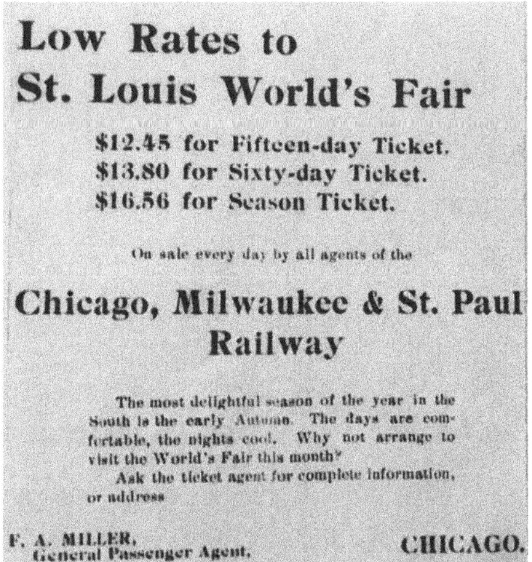

The promotion and marketing of concrete and concrete block at the St. Louis World's Fair was not lost on Mineral Point stone mason Charles Curtis and other Mineral Point businessmen. Several 1909 Mineral Point papers announced the organization of the Mineral Point Concrete Construction Company.

Charles Curtis.
Mineral Point Library Archives

Iowa County Democrat, September 23, 1909

A NEW INDUSTRY FOR MINERAL POINT

THE CONCRETE CONSTRUCTION COMPANY ORGANIZED

The making of cement blocks will shortly be one of the industries of Mineral Point. A company has been organized for this purpose, and officers have been elected. The works will be located just east of the railway depot. It is expected that operations will be begun in about a week.

It is hoped that the undertaking will prove a success and give employment to a goodly number of men. The company is incorporated for $5,000.00 and is composed of ten members: Following are the officers elected at the meeting of the company held on Friday evening, Sept 17...

Mineral Point Tribune, September 23, 1909

NEW ENTERPRISE LAUNCHED

TO BE KNOWN AS THE MINERAL POINT CONCRETE CONSTRUCTION COMPANY

READY FOR OPERATION IN ABOUT A MONTH

At a meeting of the promoters held in this city last Friday, the 17th, the Mineral Point Construction Company was duly organized by the election of the following officers:

President—Charles Curtis.

Vice President—Geo. S. Huxtable.

Secretary—J. B. Reynolds.

Treasurer—A.G. Wilkinson.

Gen'l. Manager—Vernon Clute

Directors—Charles Curtis, J. B. Reynolds, Geo. S. Huxtable, A. B. Wilkinson, Charles Wonn and V. J. Clute.

This company is incorporated for $5,000.00 and is composed of ten members, most all Mineral Point citizens or have been.

The works are to be located just east of the railroad depot, near the site of the old Butler dam. It is calculated that active operations will be begun in about a week.

A manufacturing establishment of this kind ought to do well in Mineral Point. The enterprise is certainly worthy of success.

Iowa County Democrat, August 5, 1909

THE COMING BUILDING MATERIAL

Concrete is composed of cement, sand, and fine rock or gravel. Its manufacture is as old as the Roman Empire, but it is only of late years that Portland cement has been known; and that the wonderful combination of cement and steel—reinforced concrete—has become an important factor in building operations, especially in supplanting structural steel. So far as the supply is concerned and likewise the value of concrete as a building material, its position as a competitor of stone or a supplement to stone in building operations is in most instances unassailable, while the reinforced concrete beam and column have, in the opinion of many engineers, great advantage for certain purposes over steel framing. The constituents of concrete are not only unlimited in quantity, but they are widely distributed, so as to be cheaply procurable in every section of the country; and when properly made it seems to be not only an equal, but in many respects the superior, of the very best building stone, excepting probably the question of appearance. Moreover, it is useful in a score of ways where stone and brick cannot be economically employed. Sand and rock or gravel are, of course, present in every State in the Union in absolutely inexhaustible quantities, and the materials for the manufacture of cement are only slightly less widely distributed and plentiful,—From "New Tests for Building Construction," by Guy Elliot Mitchell, in American Review of Reviews for August.

Mineral Point has a reputation for its beautiful rock buildings. Those will never be lost, but with the founding of the Mineral Point Concrete Construction Company in 1909, building with quarried rock would give way to building with manufactured concrete block.

Mineral Point Tribune, October 7, 1909

The Mineral Point Concrete Construction Company, a new enterprise just launched, is about ready to supply almost anything in the cement line.

Mineral Point Tribune, January 20, 1910

THE MINERAL POINT CONCRETE CONSTRUCTION COMPANY

is now prepared to make contracts for Cement Posts, Building Blocks, or any kind of cement work for the coming season. Will make bids for the blocks separate for building, or will make bids for the blocks and laying same in buildings or silos. Also intends to keep a line of sidewalk blocks, porch blocks and chimney blocks. For particulars and estimates see CHARLES CURTIS, Pres.

The Mineral Point Concrete Construction Company was located on 1/3 of an acre, a short distance up Darlington Road from the railroad depot. Years earlier, a large portion of this site was covered by the Butler Mill Pond, which disappeared when the mill dam washed out in 1890. The company's south property line followed the right of way of the Mineral Point and Northern Railway, and the plant was able to take delivery of equipment and raw materials such as sand, gravel and Portland cement by train.

The triangle on this aerial photograph shows where the one-third acre owned by the company was located on Darlington Road.

This circa 1918 photo shows the Mineral Point Concrete Construction Company with cement blocks stacked in their yard. The Winona Oil Company fuel tanks are shown a short distance farther up the road.

Billy Gilman Collection, Mineral Point Library Archives

Iowa County Democrat, April 21, 1910

ADDITION TO COLD STORAGE PLANT

The Glauber-Laing Company are making improvements to their Cold Storage Plant in the city. The addition which is being built is 24 x 30 feet. It is of cement blocks manufactured by the Mineral Point Concrete Construction Company.

Iowa County Democrat, May 12, 1910

CONTRACT LET

FOR 40,000 SQUARE FEET OF CEMENT WALKS

PETITION FOR NEW STREET

TWO NEW LINES OF SIDEWALKS ON DOTY AND DODGE STREETS

MINERAL POINT CONCRETE CONSTRUCTION COMPANY, SIDEWALKS 9 3/4C PER SQ. FT., CROSSINGS 12 1/2C PER SQ. FT., 2 FT. CURB AND GUTTER 55C. LINEAL FT

The Mineral Point Concrete Construction Company was a homegrown industry that was adding new products for contractors to build with. Not only were they manufacturing many kinds of building block, they were making concrete mailbox posts and fence posts. A new machine was installed at the company that was turning out the *best posts made that would last forever.* The company was designing and building garages, cellars, barns, silos and homes that were said to be *pleasing in appearance, dry and healthful, dependable, fire-safe, storm-safe, permanent and economical. Specimens of its good products can be seen on nearly every street in the city, and many towns surrounding.*

Iowa County Democrat, October 20, 1910

Mrs. Thomas Gribble's new residence, to be erected on the William Coad homestead lot on High Street, will be built of cement blocks manufactured by the Mineral Point Concrete Construction Company. Charles Curtis and other masons for the company is building the walls.

Charles Curtis built this home at 323 High Street in 1910 for Mrs. Thomas Gribble. John Sharp 2021

Iowa County Democrat, October 20, 1910

The walls of George Huxtable's new residence on Wisconsin Street are now nearly up and show that the building will present a fine appearance. The material is granolithic blocks manufactured by the Mineral Point Concrete Construction Company.

John Sharp 2019

George Huxtable was vice president of the Mineral Point Concrete Construction Company when his eye-catching granolithic cement block home was built in 1910. Commercial rock buildings and Mineral Point homes similar to this were often built with quarried limestone or sandstone rock prior to the introduction of concrete block in 1909.

Iowa County Democrat, October 20, 1910

A SUCCESSFUL PLANT

THE MINERAL POINT CONCRETE CONSTRUCTION COMPANY

do a large business in manufacturing concrete building materials and in construction work. Their shipments are large, and as their work gives excellent satisfaction their business is bound to grow.

Mineral Point Tribune, April 27, 1911

Have you visited the Concrete company's works located just east of the depot and inspected the fine assortment of blocks they are turning out? When you consider no rot, no paint, warm in the winter, cool in the summer, it pays to consider well what kind of material you use in your construction. When you build with concrete you build for a lifetime.

Mineral Point Tribune, March 7, 1912

Mr. L. C. Stair, the popular manager of the Eastman Lumber Co., has resigned his position, and the coming season will devote all his time to the interests of the Mineral Point Concrete Construction Company.

Mineral Point Tribune, May 9, 1912

ERECTION OF STORE HOUSE AND OFFICE

The Mineral Point Concrete Company has decided on erecting a storehouse and office at the plant which is located just east of the depot. The business of this company is growing rapidly, and deservedly so. The quality of the blocks turned is good and the style attractive, and the same are in great demand. It is evident that the new board of directors made a wise selection when they elected Mr. L. C. Stair as general manager.

People who intend erecting any kind of a building should not forget to examine the output of the company. Prices are so reasonable you will be surprised how little it costs.

Iowa County Democrat, August 1, 1912

DON'T CUT VALUABLE TIMBER

FOR FENCE POSTS that will last at most only a few years. Build that fence of concrete posts. They will not rot. They cannot burn. They will last forever.

The Mineral Point Concrete Company has installed a new fence post machine and are turning out the best posts made. Leave your orders now.

Mineral Point Concrete Company.

Geo. S. Huxtable, Pres.
L.C. Stair, Sec. Manager.

Iowa County Democrat, November 6, 1913

THE NEW CHURCH AT PLEASANT VIEW

Rev. William Croft informs the Democrat that work on the new church building at Pleasant View is progressing nicely. The walls are of cement block and the Mineral Point Concrete Construction Company have a contract and have a large force of men pushing the work along rapidly. The fine new building will add greatly to Pleasant View.

The Pleasant View Community Church is located on the southeast corner of County DD and Pleasant View Road in the Town of Mineral Point, Wisconsin. This small vernacular-style church has a pointed arch at the front gable end and is built with concrete corner quoins, lintels and rock-faced 7 1/2" x 24" concrete block.

John Sharp 2021

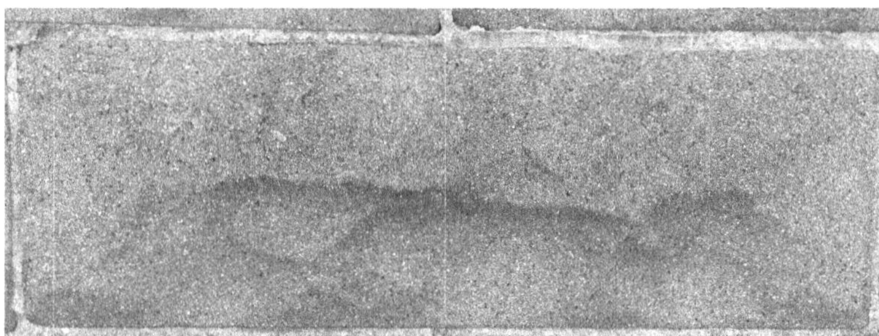

Close up of rock-faced concrete block used to build the Pleasant View Community Church.

In addition to doing a large business in manufacturing concrete building materials and doing construction work, the Mineral Point Concrete Construction Company had a crushing plant that produced crushed limestone for concrete, road work and fertilizing purposes.

Mineral Point Tribune, April 15, 1915

CONCRETE COMPANY INCREASES CAPACITY

The Mineral Point Concrete Co. has equipped their crushing plant so as to turn out daily about one hundred and fifty tons of crushed limestone for concrete and road work and fertilizer purposes. They are installing air drills and building tracks for loading cars for shipment. When the plant is in complete running order, including the well-established concrete construction branch, from ten to fifteen men will be given steady employment.

What appears to be crushed limestone piles near the top of this circa 1927 aerial photograph may be what was left of the company's rock crushing operation. The concrete company was located along Darlington Road just to the left of these piles. It is possible the company quarried rock from the old "Depot Quarry" located just to the south across Mineral Point Creek. An article in the June 2, 1921 *Tribune* stated: *They had a stone quarry near the works from which they secured rock and crushed it for street building.*

Wisconsin Historical Society Library Archives

Iowa County Democrat, December 2, 1915

PULVERIZED LIMESTONE

FOR ALFALFA AND CLOVER!

A FALL CLEAN-UP!

We have on hand about 300 tons of that High Grade Mineral Point Pulverized Limestone which assays 98 percent in lime. To clean up the lot our price will be $1.00 per ton at plant, or $1.25 per ton F. O. B. Cars.

Also about 400 concrete posts at 30c, and 15,000 Concrete Brick at $14.00 per M.

Write or Phone the Mineral Point Concrete Construction Company

Geo. S. Huxtable, Gen'l Mgr.

Mineral Point Tribune, April 13, 1916

WORTHY OF ENCOURAGEMENT

Do the citizens realize and appreciate that in this town we have an enterprise in which those behind it have already put in over $6,000? Reference is made to the Mineral Point Concrete Co., an enterprise that is sure to grow and employ several people if properly encouraged. This fact should be remembered.

Iowa County Democrat, March 20, 1919

THE CITY COUNCIL

Alderman Shepard reported on proposition of Concrete Construction Co. in regard to material for streets and recommended that city purchase glass rock from said Company according to bid.

Moved by Alderman Horn that recommendation be accepted and city purchase rock from M. P. Construction Co. according to bid.

Motion carried

Iowa County Democrat, March 22, 1917

A GROWING HOME INDUSTRY

"The business of the Mineral Point Concrete Construction Company has grown to such proportions that the present plant is inadequate to meet the demands for products. At a meeting of the directors of the company held in this city, Saturday, March 10, it was voted to increase the capital stock from $5,000 to $15,000, in order to properly equip the plant to meet the ever-increasing demand for blocks and crushed stone. They will put upon the market 70 shares of stock at $100 per share. The managers feel that the business has passed the experimental stage and is now on a solid basis. The plant will open up April 1st. There are orders already on the books sufficient to keep it going until the middle of the summer. This is the sixth year since the organization of the company. It is a home industry that adds very materially to the business of the town. Specimens of its good products can be seen in nearly every street in the city, and in many towns surrounding.

The officers of the company are: George S. Huxtable, president; George Goetsche, secretary; A. W. Wilkinson, treasurer

Mineral Point Tribune, March 25, 1920

A CONCRETE HOME IS THE FIRST STEP TO INDEPENDENCE...

HOMES ARE JUDGED BY INTELLIGENT PEOPLE UPON MOST OF THE FOLLOWING MERITS:

PLEASING APPEARANCE	**FIRE-SAFE**	**ECONOMICAL**
DRY AND HEALTHFUL	**STORM-SAFE**	
DEPENDABLE	**PERMANENT**	

The many friends who have built of our products know that all the above are realized in their concrete house.

Because of the fact that we have never had one complaint, due to inferior material, we expect to build more homes this season than ever before.

Under all conditions our products have stood the most severe tests both in quality and workmanship.

Allow us to help you with whatever building you may have to do.

MINERAL POINT CONCRETE CONSTRUCTION COMPANY

Mineral Point Tribune, 3/11/1920

Concrete Products

Are cheaper in cost and better in quality than any other building material you can buy. You would not think of throwing your money into a fire, so why build your homes of materials which create fires? Our products are fireproof.

We will design for you any concrete house you may wish so that your ideas for your home will be as you have so long planned. Beautiful, convenient and permanent. This service costs you nothing.

Last season we sold over 35,000 block, not including the building trim and porch work. Our output this season will have to be double to take care of the demand.

Think it over and place your order at once.

Mineral Point Concrete Construction Co.

Mineral Point Tribune, 4/22/1920

The above 1920 ads placed in the *Mineral Point Tribune* by the Mineral Point Concrete Construction Company were some of the last ads placed by the company. Sadly, the Company came to a violent

end on May 30th, 1921, when dynamite kept in the company storehouse on Darlington Road exploded and completely destroyed the plant.

Mineral Point Tribune, June 2, 1921

BANG!!

AND OUR CITIZENS JUMP FROM SLEEP TO FEET

At a young hour of Monday morning of this week—just a little before 3 o'clock—an awful bang jostled our city and caused its denizens to leap from sleep to feet, dazed, bewildered.

It was soon learned that an explosion of dynamite had taken place at the Cement and Concrete Works located a short distance east of the depot, on the site of the old Butler dam.

The explosion shook practically every building in the city and some located miles away. Eight large plate glass windows of business houses were shaken from their frames and fell to a broken heap, while more than that number of large double strength panes of business places met a similar fate, and a number of broken window lights throughout the residence section is estimated from 250 up, including the forty in the fourth ward school building.

Within the structure, one largely of cement sides and ends with lumber roof, where the explosion took place, a hole was torn in the ground about six feet deep and twelve feet wide at the top.

Mystery surrounds the cause. It is certainty that fire raged at the works about fifteen minutes before the explosion. Was it incendiarism, or was it resultant from a visit of some gasoline purloiner, (gasoline in tank being adjacent thereto), or was it purely accident? Because of the hour when it occurred and the fact that heretofore there had been signs of somebody having broken in and taken gasoline, it is possible the explosion is the result of another visitation of that kind.

It is understood that some of the plate glass was insured, but to replace what was broke through out (sic) the city will take $1,500 or more, so (say) those who have been figuring the claim.

George Huxtable and his nephew, Wilton Huxtable, conducted the concrete works and their loss is quite heavy, as the building, machinery, etc., therein are completely wrecked. They having a stone quary [sic] near the works from which they secured rock and crushed it for street building, using dynamite to break loose the rock at the quary (sic), accounts for the dynamite being where it was in quantity permissible by law.

The fact that no person was injured in the least is a blessing.

In an interview with Lois Holland on March 4, 2009, Lois reminisced with me about her days growing up on the family farm east of Mineral Point along Highway 39. She told me about riding her pony Spot down Darlington Road on her way to school, and how she stopped at the rock bridge on Mineral Point Creek on the way home after school to water Spot. She also told me there was a cement block factory on Darlington Road in the 1920s run by a Huxtable. Most interesting of all, Lois remembers how the explosion of the factory woke her late one night and how a car with its lights out sped past her house, heading in the direction of Madison. Lois would have been 14 years young in 1921 when the plant blew up.

> ***Wisconsin State Journal,* May 31, 1921**
>
> **EXPLOSION ROCKS MINERAL POINT**
>
> **HUSTABLE (SIC) COMPANY WAREHOUSE**
>
> **COMPLETELY WRECKED**
>
> **AS DYNAMITE EXPLODES:**
>
> **LOSS ESTIMATED AT $12,000**
>
> MINERAL POINT—A dynamite explosion that shook the town and shattered scores of windows completely wrecked the Hustable (sic) Construction company building early Monday morning, causing a loss of $11,000 to $12,000. Machinery inside the building was demolished by the blast. No one was killed or injured as far as is known. The explosion was heard fully 10 miles.
>
> The cause of the explosion is still conjectural, although the mysterious midnight visits of a prowler are believed to have a direct connection with the accident.
>
> Some person, probably attempting to steal gasoline stored in the room with the dynamite had been in the building two or three times before, according to the Hustables (sic). About 20 minutes before the explosion, which occurred at 2:35 a. m., a fire was seen in the building. Shortly afterward, according to the story told by farmers, a Ford runabout, lights extinguished and speeding in the direction of Madison was revealed by the glare from the explosion. The car had also been seen in the city shortly before.
>
> It is thought the supposed thief in some way ignited the gasoline. The blaze reached the dynamite, causing the blast. The police here are working on the case in an attempt to trace the midnight prowler.
>
> The Hustable (sic) Construction company is the dynamite agent here for the DuPont Powder company.

In the March 17, 1910 *Iowa County Democrat*, the paper quoted an article from the Highland Press telling how George Huxtable was in town selling dynamite and blasting caps, another of the many items sold by the Concrete Construction company.

> *Highland Press: George S. Huxtable was here Tuesday from Mineral Point selling powder and blasting supplies and brought along some samples of cement blocks turned out by the*

Mineral Point Concrete Construction Company. Concrete blocks are the coming material for building purposes. Mr. Huxtable is interested in the company and certainly has a good article to show up.

Iowa County Democrat, June 2, 1921

GREAT EXPLOSION

AT THE WORKS OF THE CONCRETE CONSTRUCTION COMPANY

DESTROYS PLANT AND DOES DAMAGE TO STORE AND OTHER BUILDINGS.

An explosion which aroused the people out of their beds at 2:30 o'clock Monday, morning, May 30th, occurred at the Mineral Point Concrete Construction plant. A fire at the place, first attracted the attention of John Connaughton, an employ (sic) at the Zinc Works. The explosion occurred before he could give the alarm of fire. It totally wrecked the Concrete plant and machinery, damaged the property of the Winona Oil Company adjoining, and shattered glass in store windows and residents.

Following is a partial list of places damaged:

On High Street. Glass in basement window of Masonic Temple broken. Priestly building—upstairs windows broken. Mauger's jewelry store—two window glass in back of building broken. The Jacko building, occupied by Jackson & Healy, large plate glass window broken. Thomas E. Coad building—plate glass in store and glass in door broken. T. S. Ryan—large plate glass in window demolished. W. H. Hack building—large plate glass broken. N. T. Martin Co. Building—large plate glass in northeast corner destroyed. Herman Wiesen building—one front window and two back windows broken. David C. Jacka building—plate glass window broken. Gerlach building—several panes of glass broken. J. H. Day—two windows in back of building broken.

On Commerce Street. Beers & Collins—large plate glass window broken. Groth & Noble—two or three panes of glass in back of building broken. Elmer Peter's building—two large plate glass windows broken. Mineral Point Laundry building—two windows, each 6 x 10 feet, entirely destroyed, and two small windows in back of building broken. James Keyes' hotel—five windows broken. R. D. Scidmore (sic)—windows on residence broken. The old Chesterfield building—nine window panes broken.

On Hoard Street. Windows broken at Henry Gillmann's, Mrs. John Miller and George Epstein's.

On Wisconsin Street. G. W. Holmes residence—large window glass broken. C. J. Lutgen's residence—three window glass broken.

On Davis Street. Half of cement block was blown by explosion to the residence of A. T. Sprang.

> On Pine Street. Slight damage was done at the residence of John Brewer. Several windows in Fourth ward school were broke.
>
> At the Depot. Office window broken open and glass in windows broken.

The sudden and abrupt end of the Mineral Point Concrete Construction Company was a shocking loss for the Mineral Point community. George Huxtable, who was an owner of the company and the district agent for the DuPont Powder Company, was so upset by the explosion that he let others handle insurance payments to owners of damaged properties.

By law, large quantities of explosives could not be stored at the Darlington Road factory. However, despite the dangers involved, smaller amounts permissible by law were kept in a storeroom at the plant to conduct work in their nearby quarry. Huxtable kept the bulk of the company's dynamite inventory in a storage magazine he owned on the opposite side of Mineral Point.

Although the 1929 Mineral Point Real Estate Assessment Roll showed the Mineral Point Concrete Construction Company was still the owner of the one-third acre the plant had been located on, the company was not rebuilt after the explosion. A January 19, 1922 *Mineral Point Tribune* story announced that George S. Huxtable was now a representative of the Central Life Insurance Company.

The Mineral Point Concrete Construction Company was in operation for almost twelve years. The business was short lived, but during that time, the town of Mineral Point and surrounding communities transitioned from building with quarried rock to concrete block. It is almost certain the homes and buildings you see with rock-faced concrete block were built between 1910 and 1921, and the concrete block was most likely manufactured by the Mineral Point Concrete Construction company, a unique and modern manufacturing company for its day.

CHAPTER 15: DARLINGTON ROAD EVENTS

The history of Darlington Road would not be complete without discussing some of the many unusual events and situations which occurred on and along the road over the years. They range from WWI soldiers marching into town on a soggy, rainy day in 1912, to a monster canvas tent being pitched near the concrete company that would seat 2,000 people for Terry's Big Uncle Tom's Cabin Tent Show. There was even talk of building a viaduct over the dangerous railroad tracks near the depot.

Entering Mineral Point from the east on Darlington Road, circa 1900. Mineral Point Library Archives

This southern "Rocky Point" of Mineral Point Hill is the gateway to Darlington Road valley. John Sharp 2018

Mineral Point Library Archives

When Darlington Road was the main highway into town and the depot was bustling with passenger and freight traffic, the Rocky Point at the end of Mineral Point Hill was a favorite place for businesses to advertise. These dapper fellows astride their trusty steeds paused for a picture in front of advertisements for "Sub Rosa Cigarros," Adler Clothing, Blue Ribbon Tobacco and M.P.Z. Co. 5-and-10-cent Mild and Sweet Cigars, Mfg. by Phillips Bros.

Danger Ahead—Railroad Crossing

After Jim Harris immigrated from England in 1850 and landed a job as a hauler transporting limestone rock a short distance down Darlington Road to the site of the new railroad depot, it had taken four long years of construction to complete the rail line between Warren, Illinois, and Mineral Point. The first train finally chugged into town on June 16th, 1857. Life in Mineral Point was going to change. Having the first train pull up to the depot created a sense of stability and importance to townspeople, and the following year the villagers voted to be incorporated as a city. Over the next several years, Mineral Point became a shipping and supply center for the southwest region.

Mineral Point Tribune, June 16, 1857

THE MINERAL POINT R. R. THROUGH AT LAST

The track of the Mineral Point Railroad is now laid to the Depot in Mineral Point, and this day, June 16th, the cars for the first time have arrived at that point. This news will be truly gratifying to a large class of our readers, and we are sure the Company will have no objections to its being made known. Four years ago, on the 30th of May the ground was first broken, and we well remember, as Col. Abner Nichols, on that occasion raised the first shovelful of earth from the track, the shout of joy that rent the air, in anticipation of a speedy completion of the project...

Mineral Point Tribune, June 30, 1857

M. P. R. R.—The Business on the Mineral Point Railroad exceeds the expectation of most of our citizens. Those who supposed "two sucker teams, by a trip once in two months, could do all the business the Rail Road would get," began to get their eyes open, and wonder where it all comes from and where it is going to. We were at the Depot on Friday last about the time the train was leaving, and saw it start out with seven freight cars well filled—three loaded with wheat, three with lead, and one with sundries. In the latter we noticed thirty barrels of crackers, for Galena, from the Bakery of S. Jenkin & Co. On Saturday the train up consisted of eight freight and one passenger car, all well filled.—The Road is doing a good business.

As the years progressed, the Darlington Road intersection with Commerce Street near the depot became one of the busiest intersections in Mineral Point. A scene of congestion and danger was created. Teamsters hauling heavy loads of goods pulled by large draft horses had to cross the tracks when coming into or leaving town. Trains were often moving back and forth on the tracks at the same time, and to add to the confusion, passengers disembarking at the depot were being loaded into stages and hacks to continue their journeys. Some train passengers hurried to cross Darlington Road and the tracks on foot, dodging trains and wagons, in an effort to secure a room for the night at the newly opened Mineral Point Hotel (Walker House). Congestion continued to grow and it became a concern for all involved in that part of town. There was talk of rerouting Darlington Road so it would not have to cross the tracks.

Mineral Point Library Archives

This circa 1881/82 photo of engine 335 was the first C.M. & St. Paul engine to come into Mineral Point. Engines such as this were a common sight at the Mineral Point railroad yards. The "Rocky Point" of Mineral Point Hill can be seen in the background.

Iowa County Democrat, April 5, 1900

COMMON COUNCIL MEETING, APRIL 3, 1900

The mayor made the following report regarding the placing of a flagman by railroad at crossing mentioned in ordinance passed Feb. 6, 1900:

To the Chicago, Milwaukee and St. Paul Railway Company:

You will please take notice that a certain ordinance (Ordinance No. 64) requiring you to keep and maintain a flagman at a certain crossing in the city of Mineral Point, was passed by the common council of said city on the 6th day of February, A. D. 1900, of which said ordinance a copy is hereto annexed, and that any violation of said ordinance will be punished as therein provided.

James Spensley,

Mayor of the City of Mineral Point.

Dated March 14, 1900

State of Wisconsin, Iowa County

Iowa County Democrat, August 3, 1905

CROSSING ON DARLINGTON ROAD NEEDED

A most important matter was brought to the attention of the (Advancement Association) meeting by President Penhallegon, and that was regarding the danger of going over the tracks at the Mineral Point depot while cars and engines are almost constantly moving back and forth over the crossings. The question of having a flagman for the crossings was considered, as was also that of changing streets, so as to avoid the railway crossings. On motion a committee, consisting of T. M. Priestly, James Brewer and W. H. Cornell, was appointed to investigate in regard to the matter and report at the next meeting of the association in September.

Iowa County Democrat, November 2, 1905

ANOTHER HIGHWAY NEEDED

The rapidly increasing railway traffic in the yards of the C. M. & St. P. And M. P. & N. Railways at Mineral Point and the ever-large traffic by team over the Darlington Road into town make another highway entrance from the east an imperative necessity for this community. It seems that such an entrance can easily be secured by opening up a street in front of the Mineral Point Hotel (Walker House), now the property of Charles Curtis. If this can be done, it ought to be done at once. There is a growing discontent among the great numbers of people who come to Mineral Point from the east and not without just cause—over the congested conditions referred to above. It is to be hoped neither the railway traffic nor the traffic by team will ever grow less; and the proper remedy is to be found in opening up another street. Another Highway is needed.

Suggestions for solving the danger and congestion problems at the Darlington Road rail crossing ranged from making a new street in front of the Mineral Point Hotel to building a viaduct over the tracks. At a March 7, 1907 meeting of the Commercial Club, a resolution requesting the St. Paul company to erect a new depot building was even introduced.

Iowa County Democrat, March 7, 1907

THE COMMERCIAL CLUB

at a special meeting on Tuesday evening, adopted a resolution, presented by E. C. Fiedler, which petitions the council to so amend ordinance 64, and so provide for its enforcement as to require the presence of a competent flagman at the depot railway crossing every week day between the hours of 7 a. m. and 7 p. m.

A motion was also adopted asking the common council to further safe guard the public by opening up a street along the west side of the Curtis property. (Walker House)

A resolution requesting the St. Paul Company to erect a new depot building was also introduced and will be acted on at the next regular meeting of the club.

At the March 14, 1907 Mineral Point common council meeting, serious and meaningful discussion and action was taken to solve the dangerous conditions at the Darlington Road rail crossing. The March 14, 1907 *Iowa County Democrat* printed the following account of the meeting and the ordinance that resulted.

Iowa County Democrat, March 14, 1907

COMMON COUNCIL DOINGS

A FLAGMAN REQUIRED AT RAILROAD CROSSING.

PROPOSED BY ORDINANCE, WHICH IS PUBLISHED.

CHARGES TO BE CONSIDERED

Mineral Point, Wisc., Mch 11, 1907 The adjourned regular meeting of the common council was held this day in the council chamber. Called to order by Mayor Osborne, Ald. Weidenfeller, Horn, Ross, Terrill, Potter, Engels. absent: Ald. Blewett, Burns.

A resolution of the Commercial club regarding the railroad crossing north of the depot presented and discussed by W. A. Jones, N. H. Snow, E. C. Fiedler and Ed Brown. The following ordinance was then introduced and upon the following aye and nay vote was adopted.

NO. 90. AN ORDINANCE

REQUIRING RAILWAY COMPANIES TO KEEP A FLAGMAN

The common council of the city of Mineral Point do ordain as follows:

Section 1. The Chicago, Milwaukee and St. Paul railway and the Mineral Point and Northern railway company are hereby required to keep and maintain, at their own residence expense, a competent flagman on all days (except Sundays) from Seven o'clock a. m. to seven o'clock p. m. at the railroad crossing just north of the railway depot in the city of Mineral Point, where the tracks of said railway companies cross the public streets at the intersection of Commerce street with the street running eastwardly from said Commerce street and commonly called the Darlington road, and it shall be the duty of said railway companies, by their flagman to reasonably signal and warn all persons about to pass over any of said crossings of danger from approaching or passing engines or cars.

Section 2. If said railway companies shall fail to comply with any of the requirements of this ordinance, said companies, and each of them, shall forfeit and pay to the city of Mineral Point the sum of fifty dollars for every such failure or neglect of duty. This ordinance shall be in force and effect from and after its passage and publication.

Section 3. Ordinance No. 64 published March 8, 1901 is hereby repealed.

Aye, Weidnfeller, Ross, Horn, Terrill, Potter, Engels. Nay, no votes.

After deliberation on the situation at the Darlington Road railroad crossing, the council unanimously voted that the railroad companies would be subject to penalties if they did not keep a competent flagman at the crossing on all days except Sunday.

Iowa County Democrat, March 28, 1907

LOCAL NEWS ITEMS

The C. M. & St. P and the M. P. & N. railway companies now have a flagman stationed at the crossing just north of the depot, whose duty it is to warn all persons about to pass over said crossing of danger from approaching engines or cars. The effort to guard against accidents from passing trains is right so far as it goes; but it is of the utmost importance that as soon as possible the city acting in conjunction with the railway companies should provide additional safety, by the construction of a viaduct or the opening up of a street in front of the Mineral Point hotel.

Iowa County Democrat, March 28, 1907

Thomas Mullen is the flagman at the depot. He signals with a white flag when the way is clear and with the red if there is any danger.

Starting in 1907 with Thomas Mullen, several men served as flagman at the C. M. & St. Paul and the Mineral Point & Northern railway crossing on Darlington Road near the depot. Some of the

Flagman on the Darlington Road railway crossing. Mineral Point Library Archives

other flagmen who directed traffic at this crossing were William Murphy (1910–1914), Frank Ivey (1919) and Edwin Millard.

Lester Dunwiddie wrote this brief sketch of Ed the flagman in his book, "Home When the Whistle Blew."

Railroads

Ed's Cabin

I am wondering how many people remember when the highway from Mineral Point to Hollandale and Darlington crossed the railroad tracks near the old depot? I think back to a little cabin beside the road just before crossing the tracks on this highway. This building was about 8 feet square. It had one window and a door with a glass in it. There was a galvanized smoke stack sticking up through the roof. This served as the chimney for the stove inside the cabin.

Lester's sketch of Ed's Cabin.

At first look, we might wonder what the cabin was standing there for. As we stood at the depot when the train arrived, we would see a short man with leather boots, dressed in a mackinaw jacket, large warm mittens, furry cap pulled down over his ears on a cold snowy winter day, step out of the cabin. This man was Ed, the crossing guard. The cabin was his home during working hours. It kept him warm in winter and dry in rainy weather. It provided some protection from the hot sun in summer.

Ed was an important workman. At times there would be several crews switching trains at the same time. There was always a line of traffic crossing the tracks. Some cars, horses pulling buggies or wagons, people walking from the depot to the hotel across the street, all needed someone to alert them of the trains approach to prevent accidents.

Ed carried a signal flag and was very watchful of the activities. He used the flag to signal the highway traffic to halt when a train was coming. There were many trains that kept Ed very busy. He worked from morning to late night, using a red lantern after sunset. During the years I remember, there was never a collision. Ed and his flag directed traffic for many years. Watching Ed come out of his cabin to stand in the heat, cold, rain or snow to protect the lives of others is one of my fondest memories. I miss Ed and his Cabin.

Mineral Point Library Archives

The flagman cabin Lester Dunwiddie wrote about is shown on the left side background of the Mineral Point Railroad Depot photo above.

The Yanks are Coming

On a rainy Friday morning, June 14, 1912, 2,200 United States soldiers marched down Darlington Road with auto trucks and four-hitch mule freight wagons carrying their supplies into Mineral Point. For residents of Mineral Point, this was a once-in-a-lifetime event, and hundreds turned out to see the soldiers and their equipment streaming into town past the depot.

The following newspaper articles and pictures captured the event and told the story.

Mineral Point Tribune, June 20, 1912

2,200 OF UNCLE SAM'S BOYS PASS THROUGH MINERAL POINT

Between 9 and 10 o'clock Friday morning 2,200 of United States soldiers and their equipment of transport service—four-mule outfits and powerful auto trucks—passed through this city, en route to Sparta. The force consisted of four companies—the 4th, 26th, 27th and 28th—the same meeting at Dubuque from Forts Crook, Snelling, Sheridan and Brady. They started from Dubuque and camped four miles southeast of this city Thursday night.

Aside from a practical outing it was one of test between mule and auto and also to try out modern arms, mode for carrying necessary equipment, etc. Unfortunately for one and all it rained every minute of the time taken up by the troops to pass through our city, including the ten minutes allowed for rest. Nevertheless, a large crowd turned out to witness and greet them, even the school children being dismissed for the purpose. It proved an exceptionally rare sight for our people, old and young, as not one in a hundred ever before saw 2,000 soldiers in line.

Mineral Point Library Archives

Iowa County Democrat, June 20, 1912

U. S. SOLDIERS

TO THE NUMBER OF OVER 2,000 CAMP NEAR MINERAL POINT

TESTING EQUIPMENTS

ON MARCH FROM DUBUQUE, IOWA, TO SPARTA, WISCONSIN.

Col. Getty with more than 2,000 soldiers of the regular army, from Forts Sheridan, Snelling, Brady, and Crook, started on Monday, June 10, from Dubuque on a March to Sparta, the purpose being to prove and compare army equipments, including powerful auto trucks.

The march from Dubuque to Mineral Point was by way of Darlington, and they reached the latter place on Wednesday. The march was continued and in the evening the soldiers camped along Darlington Road, about five miles south of Mineral Point. Tents were pitched in regular army fashion, with outposts and sentries at all hours.

In the morning the soldiers broke camp and the main body reached Mineral Point at about nine o'clock, continuing the March towards Dodgeville.

Later some of the soldiers returned here with the auto trucks and wagons for the purpose of purchasing provisions of various kinds.

The journey from Dubuque to this was made under trying circumstances. Rains had made the roads muddy, and the auto trucks were given a severe test. Two of them stuck by the way, and two reached here, as did the transport wagons being drawn by six mules.

Mineral Point Library Archives

Capt. Williams, who has been making experiments with the auto trucks for hauling provisions and equipments on marches of the regular army, says: "The one and a half (ton) auto truck is a success, and I believe will replace the mule, but the larger trucks must be made lighter before they will be available for army use."

The March of the provisional regiment was an object lesson to the people who are unaccustomed to witnessing the movement of troops. Nearly all of the soldiers were afoot, but they had with them in all about one hundred head of horse and some of these were very fine animals.

The march of the soldiers over the muddy roads was a trying one, each soldier being required to carry about 70 pounds of baggage. The men however, were soldierly in their bearing.

Mineral Point Tribune, July 4, 1912

As is generally understood those two thousand soldiers of Uncle Sam's who recently passed through Mineral Point were pressing on toward Madison. They got there, or most of them did, but our capital city saw a touch of real soldier life when twenty-five deserters were brought back to camp in irons. Since leaving Dubuque, it is said that 200 have deserted. Some went to Fort Sheridan and others to Fort Snelling and still others to Sparta to avoid a 200-mile march on foot.

Having 2,200 United States soldiers with mule teams and auto trucks round the point of Mineral Point Hill on Darlington Road and pass by the depot was a once-in-a-lifetime event for the town. What a sight. I wish I had been there.

Turning Turtle (and other unusual mishaps along the road)

Mineral Point Tribune, July 15, 1875

SERIOUS ACCIDENT

On Monday afternoon as Mrs. Hoffman, of Waldwick, was returning from this city, accompanied by her son, they drove into the water near Butler's dam to water the team. The boy walked out upon the tongue to un-rein the horses. At that moment a snake sprang into the water in front of them, at which they took fright and whirled around throwing Mrs. Hoffman from the wagon. The boy clung to the reins, but the runaway was complete, and the wagon was dashed to pieces. The unfortunate woman was picked up and taken to the house of a friend, where she is being cared for, but she is injured internally, and there is little chance of her recovery.

Mineral Point Tribune, April 29, 1915

A DANGEROUS PRACTICE

Last Friday as Mrs. Charles Allen was driving into town she narrowly escaped being struck by a stray bullet. She had just reached the old town hall when a bullet whistled over her horse's head, bringing the faithful animal to a standstill; and a little further another bullet passed over in close proximity. Some boys down in the hollow were shooting a rifle, and their shots went wild. The careless handling of firearms is a most dangerous practice.

Mineral Point Tribune, July 13, 1916

A dead drunk, all alone in an auto anchored crossways of the public highway near the old town hall, demanded Marshal Thrasher's attention Tuesday evening between 8 and 9 o'clock. The fellow claims to be of Madison.

Iowa County Democrat, July 20, 1916

"AN OVERLOADED CAR DRIVER"

Last Thursday evening Roy Thrasher, city Marshall, was called out on to the Darlington Road, by reports of a man who was handling an automobile in a reckless manner. Near the sight of the old town hall he found the car turned squarely across the road; and the driver lying in it and completely overcome with liquor. Both driver and car were brought to town and kept overnight. Wednesday morning, both Justice Hankins and Justice Kuelling being at Madison, administrating first aid to the Jeffris and Philipp movement, the driver was taken to Dodgeville and tried before Justice T. H. Arthur, who posted a fine and costs.

Iowa County Democrat, March 3, 1928

HORSE AND AUTO INJURED IN COLLISION FRIDAY NIGHT

A horse owned by William Hewitt was struck in the left hind quarter and its leg broken Friday night about eight o'clock when struck by an auto. The horse had strayed a long distance from the owner's home. The mishap occurred about one hundred yards past the first bridge on the Darlington Road.

Ulmont Healy, who was driving the car down the hill on which the accident occurred, was unable to see the horse because blinded by the bright lights of a car coming up the hill. The radiator of the auto was smashed.

Saturday morning the city team removed the injured animal.

At a Town of Mineral Point annual meeting held April 5, 1881, an order and by-law was adopted that made it unlawful for any cattle, horned animals, horses, sheep, swine, mules, jennies or asses to run at large in any of the highways of said town, under penalty not to exceed ten dollars in any one case for a violation of this order. Public pounds were established, and poundmasters were appointed. John E. Suthers was appointed poundmaster at Graysville.

Iowa County Democrat, August 2, 1928

TIRE BLOW OUT CAUSES CAR TO TURN TURTLE

(PLEASANT VIEW COR.)

A sedan belonging to Mrs. Emil Boeing of Dodgeville, turned turtle on the Hollandale Road near the Harker & Humbert slaughter pen when a tire blew out.

Mrs. Boeing and son, Miss Ella Thomas, Mrs., Josiah Thomas and Mrs. Charles Thomas were in the car when the accident occurred. They were returning to their home after spending the afternoon at home of Mr. and Mrs. Everett Thomas. All the occupants escaped injury except Mrs. Josiah Thomas, who was so unfortunate to have an arm broken.

Authors note: Even though this auto mishap occurred further out of town on the Hollandale Road, these colorful words describing an automobile "turned turtle" have not left my mind, so hence, I am including it in this section on Darlington Road mishaps.

Special Events

Mineral Point Tribune, July 28, 1910

UNCLE TOM'S CABIN

Terry's Uncle Tom's Cabin Company, which showed to a crowded tent last Saturday evening, gave one of the best performances we have witnessed under a canvas. The play was appropriately staged, the cast well balanced and the orchestra superior to that of the average company. The tableaux, Rock of Ages, which is the scene given most attention in this play, has never been equaled here. Buck and wing dancing, clogs and hoe downs, together with a genuine cake walk, were the leading specialties. A return engagement here will secure a crowded tent.—Daily Telegraph, Atlantic, Iowa.

This company will appear in Mineral Point on Saturday, July 30.

Mineral Point Tribune, July 28, 1910

GET THE TERRY HABIT. AFTER THE MINNOWS COMES THE WHALE.

20 YEARS—THE EVERLASTING SUCCESS—20 YEARS

TERRY'S BIG

UNCLE TOM'S CABIN

TENT SHOWS

THE KING AND MONARCH OF THEM ALL—FOREVER FOREMOST—NEWEST EDITION OF THE OLDEST HIT

Exhibiting in monster canvas tent, seating 2,000 people. Two Bands, forty Actors, Singers, Dancers, Specialty People. 15 Colored people, Grand Cake Walk, Herd of Shetland Ponies and Donkeys—Pack of Ferocious, Siberian Bloodhounds—Gorgeous Scenic and Electrical effects—Cowboys' Quartette.

MINERAL POINT, SATURDAY JULY 30

HEAR	***SEE***
The Greatest Military Band	The Ice Choked Ohio River
The Soloist Orchestra	The Home of Phibeas Fletcher
The Louisiana Quartette	The Chimes Wagon of 100 Bells
The Southern Songs	The Rocky Pass
The Jubilee singers	Slave market of New Orleans
The Augmented Chorus	The Grand Transformation Scene
The Plantation Melodies	The Legrees Red River Plantation
Jones' Concert Band	The Hindoo Snake Dance
Jockmans Orchestra	McCann the noted Hoop Roller
Parade at 12:00 noon	**Band Concert at 7 p.m.**

PERFORMANCE AT NIGHT ONLY

Doors open at 7:30 p. m. Performance at 8:00 p. m.

General Admission 35c. Children under ten, 25c.

WANTED—15 boys at show cars at 11 a. m. Also 3 working men, steady work.

Iowa County Democrat, August 4, 1910

TERRY'S UNCLE TOM'S CABIN COMPANY

The drawing power of advertising was forcibly illustrated by Terry's Uncle Tom's Cabin show last Saturday night. The event was widely advertised, and the tent was pitched over by the Mineral Point Concrete Construction works, across the railway tracks from the town; but more townspeople attended than had crossed those tracks in a generation, and all the county roads led to Uncle Tom's Cabin show.

Sport Shooting Events

The sport of trap shooting captured the interest of American sports shooters when James Graham of Long Lake, Illinois, won the gold medal for trap shooting at the 1912 Summer Olympics in Stockholm, Sweden.

Two years later, the American Amateur Trapshooting Association was formed with John Philip Sousa at its helm, and in 1916, the Mineral Point Trap Shooting Club was organized, establishing the club's shooting grounds opposite the concrete construction plant on Darlington Road. By 1917, trap shooting had become a social and recreational activity and was considered a patriotic sport. Wisconsin had over 100 clubs, including the Mineral Point club.

Iowa County Democrat, August 3, 1916

M. P. TRAP SHOOTING CLUB

All sportsmen are cordially invited to attend a meeting to be held at Public Meeting Room in Farmers and Citizens Bank Friday evening, Aug 4. An object of this meeting is to consider the proposition of organizing a Trap Shooting club. Such an organization will be a distinct advantage to our city. We want you to cooperate with us. Committee

Mineral Point Tribune, September 7, 1916

AFFILIATED WITH NATIONAL ORGANIZATION

W. S. Lesley, secretary of the Mineral Point Trap Shooting club, has received word that the local club has been admitted to affiliation with the American Amateur Trapshooters' Association.

This permits the local club to hold shoots for proficiency medals.

James Graham

Mineral Point Tribune, September 14, 1916

BEGINNER'S SHOOT

The opening shoot of the Mineral Point Trap Shooting club will be held on their grounds, opposite the Concrete Co. Plant, Thursday afternoon, Sept. 14, at 1:30 o'clock.

The public is cordially invited to attend. Admission free.

Iowa County Democrat, September 28, 1916

TRAP-SHOOTING FRIDAY AFTERNOON

Trap shooting at the Mineral Point Trap Shooting Club grounds FRIDAY afternoon at 2 p.m. everybody come and bring a friend.

M. P. TRAP SHOOTING CLUB.

Mineral Point Tribune, July 12, 1917

4th of July Trap Shoot

The trap shooting event, conducted under the auspices of the Mineral Point Trap Shooting club on the morning of July 4th, proved to be a spirited and interesting contest. Frank Van Matre won first prize and in a few cases a lady shooter scored higher than some of the local enthusiasts. The score:

	Shot at	Broke
Frank Van Matre	75	66
W. G. Martin	"	62
Chas. Skinner	"	59
J. P. Harris, Jr.	"	58
R. E. Orton	"	57
Ed Martin	"	49

The first recorded trap shooting events in the United States took place in Ohio in 1831. Before the advent of organized shooting competitions, Mineral Point shooters gathered to test their skills with firearms. Not all shooting matches were organized or civilized, as recorded by this September 22, 1853 *Wisconsin Tribune* article.

Wisconsin Tribune, September 22, 1853

THREE MEN SHOT

On Saturday afternoon last, at a Shooting match near Musgrove's Furnace, (Merry Christmas mine building) in this town, three men were shot through the legs by a discharge of a gun thrown violently upon the ground by a man in a state of intoxication—There appeared to have been some slight misunderstanding, which threw this man into a rage, whereupon

> he threw his gun with such force as to break the stock, and cause the discharge. From appearances there must have been several balls in the gun, as one was taken from the leg of the person who threw the gun, another was hit in three places below the knee, and the third was wounded near the knee, while a boy was slightly grazed near the thigh. There was a large number of persons standing at the time, and the great wonder is that more damage was not done. Here is another argument in favor (of) a Prohibitory Liquor Law, and an evidence of the danger of firearms in the hands of drunken men.

Because Darlington Road was the main road into and out of Mineral Point from the east prior to 1948, it was a busy place. Bottlenecks were created by trains blocking the road near the depot, vehicles were coming and going to the many businesses located along the road and congestion was created by the special events that took place. Today, Old Darlington Road is a quiet city road with residences replacing businesses and no special events are happening to speak of.

ABOUT THE AUTHOR

John Sharp, whose persistence and diligence made possible this historic volume, was born at the Oakland California Army Hospital in 1944 and later grew up in Salt Lake City, Utah, and Park City, Utah. His interest in American history and the early West began in his youth when his father bought an old log cabin homestead near Park City. He spent many summers fixing the place up and roaming the Wasatch Mountains above Park City, poking around ghost-mining camps. Along the way, he became interested in colored, handmade glass bottles and would accompany a desert rat antique dealer friend of his to Alta, Utah, to dig the old outhouse holes for bottles. Another passion of John's was wood carving. He carved historic western signs like "Boot Hill," "Long Branch Saloon," and "Bull Durham Tobacco" and then traded them for western relics. Wood carving became his life's work.

After graduating from the University of Utah in 1969 with a Bachelor of Science in History, he bought a run-down building in Park City, which after some research turned out to be one of the only buildings on Park City's Main Street to survive the great 1898 fire that burned Park City to the ground. John fixed the falling-down building up, and in 1972, he and his wife, Jennifer, opened an art gallery where she painted and sold her watercolors, and he carved and sold his western woodcarvings.

In 1979, John and Jennifer pulled stakes and moved to Mineral Point, Wisconsin. Jennifer was from Wisconsin, and it was her turn to decide where to live. They bought the James Spensley house west of town and began another restoration project, and in 1986, Jennifer bought the 1829 John F. O'Neill building on Commerce Street that she and John restored into another art gallery. After living on the Spensley farm for eighteen years, they pulled stakes once again and moved back to the West to Astoria, Oregon. A year on the beautiful Oregon Coast at the mouth of the Columbia River could not dampen their memories of Mineral Point and old friends. John and Jennifer pulled stakes one last time and returned home to Mineral Point in 2000.

Jennifer again discovered a diamond in the rough, and they bought the Old Darlington Road property to build a home. Thus began the 10-year research that has culminated with the story of "Along the Old Darlington Road."

Printed in the United States
by Baker & Taylor Publisher Services